*To the next generation of Mediterranean
cooks to whom I pass down these recipes –
my three angels, Vasili, Sofia and Ruby,
and their cousins, Dylan, Ellis, Eliana and Billy.*

GLUTEN-FREE MEDITERRANEAN

HELEN TZOUGANATOS

plum. Pan Macmillan Australia

CONTENTS

Introduction

I was raised on a Mediterranean diet. Our pantry was always stocked with quality extra-virgin olive oil, tomatoes, kalamata olives, artisanal cheese, fresh herbs and an abundance of dried spices. With these staples, my mother could whip up myriad recipes, from express mid-week pastas to slow-cooked hearty stews. Most recipes started with a drizzle of robust organic extra-virgin olive oil – pressed by hand at my yiayia's green olive groves on the beautiful island of Crete – into a hot pan. To finish, extra oil was drizzled over the dish for presentation and a boost of olive flavour.

As a child I was responsible for generously drizzling olive oil over our rustic Greek salad at the dinner table. I would also slather my hands with this liquid gold to roll biscuit dough with my mum, the oil helping to prevent the dough from sticking to our hands. Butter was used sparingly in our house and was normally reserved for desserts and pastries. Even then, there was always an olive oil version of our favourite biscuit, cake or pastry.

Growing up in Sydney's multicultural inner west I was fortunate to be surrounded by migrant neighbours from various countries spanning the Mediterranean. My Lebanese neighbours taught me the secret to the best Mejadra (page 69), the Cypriots across the road were the first to introduce me to Koupes (page 160) and Haloumi Bread (page 22), and my mother often exchanged Greek syrupy sweets for Pistachio Biscotti (page 198) and Olive and Rosemary Focaccia (page 20) with the Italians down the street. Regardless of which Mediterranean country the recipe derived from (and this was often a source of competitive debate!), they all shared a few common threads: olive oil, plant rich, nutrient dense and prepared from scratch with lots of love.

So, what exactly is a Mediterranean diet? Why is it associated with longevity of life and consistently ranked as the healthiest in the world? Essentially, countries that adopt a Mediterranean diet use olive oil as their primary fat source, with some added healthy fats from nuts, seeds and fish. Fresh fruit and vegetables, legumes and pulses are eaten in abundance, along with moderate amounts of dairy and smaller amounts of red meat. This healthy eating pattern has been proven to help reduce cardiovascular disease, the risk of stroke, cognitive illnesses and type 2 diabetes. It also helps to maintain a healthy weight.

Two of the five 'Blue Zones' in the world are located in the Mediterranean: Sardinia in Italy and Ikaria in Greece. On these islands people have the lowest rates of chronic disease and live longer than anywhere else in the world. Their diet is primarily plant based and low in saturated fat and processed foods. Natural movement, low stress and an occasional glass of red wine also help.

Although veganism is not common in Mediterranean countries, most people's diets are surprisingly high in vegan and vegetarian dishes. Historically, many Mediterraneans could not afford the luxury of meat, so they had to make do with what they had. Peasant dishes from ancient times still form the cornerstone of their simple weekly meals. In Greece, vegan dishes are also popular due to traditional periods of fasting. During Lent, meat, dairy and eggs are eliminated from the diet.

Where does gluten fit into all of this? Thankfully, the Mediterranean diet is primarily naturally gluten free as it is based on whole, unprocessed foods. The most significant challenges when eating gluten free on a Mediterranean diet are bakery items and the sneaky breadcrumbs often found in meatballs. But with some simple swaps your focaccia will be soft and bouncy again, and I will teach you the trick to achieving the crispiest honey-drenched Loukoumades (page 168).

Given that more than half of those who follow a gluten-free diet also avoid dairy, the majority of the recipes in this book are dairy free or can easily be made dairy free. To help you identify which recipes are suitable to your dietary needs, look out for the following categories:

DF = DAIRY FREE

DFO = DAIRY-FREE OPTION

GF = GLUTEN FREE

V = VEGETARIAN

VO = VEGETARIAN OPTION

VG = VEGAN

VGO = VEGAN OPTION

I hope this book allows you to reintroduce foods into your diet that you have not been able to eat or enjoy in years – nobody wants to feel excluded at the family dinner table. I love witnessing the reaction of my family and friends when I serve them a slice of syrup cake that is just as good, if not better, than the 'gluten' version. Seeing the surprise and delight on their faces is always so rewarding.

One final note: the Mediterranean diet is more than just a way of eating; it's a lifestyle. Take pleasure in drizzling an extra splash of olive oil over your pasta or drinking a glass of red wine with friends. Foster social connections; food cultivates a bond with others, so please cook and share these recipes with your loved ones. Your palate and soul will be so much richer.

Kali orexi, buon appetito, buen provecho and bel hana wel shefa!

The gluten-free
Mediterranean pantry

ARTISANAL CHEESE

GREEK FETA & MANOURI

Authentic Greek feta is labelled 'PDO' (Protected Designation of Origin) and produced using sheep's and goat's milk from specific areas in Greece with high biodiversity and special soil and weather conditions. The best-quality feta will always have a stark white colour and creamy texture; avoid imitation 'feta-style' cheese with a yellow tinge and brittle texture.

Manouri is a semi-soft, white milk-whey cheese that is a by-product of the production of feta. It is a milder option than parmigiano reggiano and is delicious grated over pasta.

HALOUMI

This salty brined cheese from Cyprus is made from sheep's and goat's milk. Haloumi has a unique firm rubbery texture, so it is suited to grilling and frying, and tastes fantastic when paired with contrasting flavours like sweet honey or acidic lemon. Cypriot Haloumi Bread (page 22) is one of the most iconic bakery items in the Mediterranean and is very easy to make, perfect for a beginner.

KEFALOTYRI, KEFALOGRAVIERA & KASSERI

These hard, salty Greek cheeses are made from sheep's or goat's milk (or both) and can often be used interchangeably. Their flavour profile is similar to Spanish manchego, which is made exclusively from sheep's milk.

PARMIGIANO REGGIANO & PECORINO

These two hard, salty Italian cheeses can generally be used interchangeably. Parmigiano reggiano is made from cow's milk and is golden, brittle and nutty. It is aged for a minimum of one year. Pecorino is made from sheep's milk and is aged for five to eight months, so it has a waxier texture and stronger grassy, tangy flavour. The rind of both cheeses can be added to soups and stews for umami flavour.

RICOTTA

A soft, moist Italian whey cheese that is low in fat and extremely versatile, ricotta can be used in sweet and savoury dishes and baking. It adds incredible moistness to my Fluffy Lemon, Ricotta and Blueberry Loaf (page 186).

CANNED TOMATOES

Canned tomatoes, rich in both flavour and the antioxidant lycopene, form the cornerstone of many Mediterranean recipes. The best-quality canned tomatoes are jammy and ripe without any additives or preservatives.

CHOCOLATE

COCOA POWDER

There are two types of cocoa powder: natural or dutch-process. Natural cocoa is light and bitter, whereas dutch-process cocoa has been alkalised to deliver a deeper colour and a more mellow flavour – ideal when you want an intensely dark colour in biscuits or a cake, like my olive oil chocolate cake (page 192).

DARK CHOCOLATE (70% COCOA)

This is what I bake with when I want a rich chocolate flavour. A lower cocoa content will deliver a less intense flavour and you will immediately taste the difference. Check the label to ensure there is no barley in the ingredients list, as barley contains gluten.

COCONUT

Organic desiccated coconut is far superior to other brands in terms of taste, texture, moisture and aroma and well worth paying a little extra for. Most supermarkets now stock organic desiccated coconut in the health-food aisle.

BAKING POWDER

To convert gluten-free plain flour to self-raising flour, simply add 2 teaspoons of baking powder per cup of plain flour. Ensure you purchase a brand of baking powder labelled 'gluten free'.

CORNFLOUR

A fine white flour derived from ground corn kernels, cornflour has a neutral flavour, so it is extremely versatile. It is a great thickening agent in sauces and will make anything fried crispier due to its high starch content. A little cornflour will make your gluten-free Loukoumades (page 168) extra crispy. Ensure you purchase a brand labelled 'gluten free' and made from 100 per cent corn, as some brands contain wheat.

GLUTEN-FREE PASTA

Today, there are many types of gluten-free pasta available. It is primarily made from a blend of corn, rice, potato and tapioca, but you can also buy high-fibre and high-protein gluten-free pulse pastas made with peas, chickpeas, beans and lentils. Whatever your preference, remember to cook your pasta in a pan of salted boiling water until just al dente so it doesn't become too mushy, and drag some starchy pasta water into your sauces to make them silkier and help the sauce cling to the pasta. Pair rich sauces like bolognese with wider, chunkier pasta shapes that can stand up to the sauce, and delicate shapes, such as thin spaghetti, with lighter sauces.

GLUTEN-FREE PLAIN FLOUR

The quality of commercial gluten-free plain flours can vary greatly. Every manufacturer has their own unique blend, aiming to mimic regular wheat flour. Some brands bake well while others will leave you with a crumbly mess. My advice is to try a few before you settle on one you like. As a general rule, you get what you pay for, with the more expensive brands delivering far superior results.

ITALIAN GLUTEN-FREE BREAD/PIZZA FLOUR

Excellent-quality Italian gluten-free bread/pizza flours contain a proprietary blend of gluten-free starches that add incredible stretch and stickiness to your dough. This flour is a must if you want to bake a fluffy gluten-free Focaccia (page 20) that tastes just as good as a regular focaccia – a gluten-free plain flour will not deliver the same results. You can find Italian gluten-free bread/pizza flour in gourmet grocers, European delis and online.

NUT MEALS

As the name suggests, nut meals are made from ground nuts like almonds, hazelnuts and pistachios. They have a slightly coarse texture and rich, nutty flavour. Nut meals are high in protein, fibre, vitamins, minerals and healthy fats, making them a great option for people following a low-carb, grain-free or paleo diet. The natural fats add incredible moistness and richness to food, quite often meaning the recipe doesn't require added fat. In my Pasta Flora (page 190), almond meal adds richness and buttery notes to the pastry.

POLENTA

Made from corn, polenta is a versatile gluten-free grain. It is a fantastic gluten-free substitute for semolina in syrupy cakes because it has a similar gritty texture that soaks up syrups beautifully (see my Revani on page 178). Polenta can also be used to form a delicious crispy crust on a cheat's spanakopita (page 37) or a rustic village bread (Bobota, page 27).

QUINOA

One of the most versatile and nutrient-dense 'superfoods' in a gluten-free pantry, quinoa is a complete protein, containing all nine essential amino acids. It is also high in fibre, magnesium, iron, potassium and antioxidants. Quinoa must be thoroughly rinsed before cooking to remove its natural saponin coating, which has a bitter taste and can be difficult to digest.

RICE

All rice is naturally gluten free. Popular Mediterranean rices include starchy arborio and carnaroli for risotto, bomba or calasparra for paella and a medium-grain or basmati rice as a basic versatile rice to serve with rich slow-cooked tomato stews.

TAPIOCA FLOUR

The most versatile flour in the gluten-free pantry is tapioca, which is derived from the cassava plant native to South America. Tapioca is good for binding, thickening and crumbing, and adds great texture to baked goods. It will make your bread bouncy, your crumb light and your sauces thicker. It is my go-to flour when crumbing fish or chicken.

FRUITS & VEGETABLES

Mediterranean cooking has a strong farm-to-table ethos. Produce is often sourced from the home garden or local grocer, so if you don't have a vegetable or herb garden, buy the freshest organic produce you can. Eating a rainbow of different fruits and vegetables means you consume a variety of nutrients and phytonutrients (small chemical compounds produced by plants that contain powerful antioxidants and help prevent cell damage in our bodies). Wild leafy greens (Horta, page 80) is one of the most antioxidant-rich vegan meals you can enjoy on a regular basis and very simple to prepare.

OLIVES

For superior flavour and texture, buy whole unpitted olives and pit them yourself. The colour of an olive depends on when it is picked and how it is cured. Unripe green olives are denser and more bitter, whereas ripe black olives are oilier and fruitier. Both contain healthy monounsaturated fats and minerals, in addition to antioxidants that possess anti-inflammatory properties. My favourite all-rounder for taste and versatility is the plump black kalamata olive, which I always have in my fridge.

HERBS & SPICES

Fresh herbs and dried spices form the flavour base of Mediterranean dishes. They also contain concentrated levels of antioxidants and have anti-inflammatory and anti-carcinogenic properties.

Mediterranean countries tend to source from the same pool of herbs and spices; however, certain spices are associated with specific regions. For example, Greek dried oregano, Spanish paprika, Lebanese sumac, Italian basil and Cypriot coriander. Below are the most common herbs and spices used in the Mediterranean kitchen.

FRESH	DRIED
BASIL	ALLSPICE
BAY LEAF	CINNAMON
CHIVES	CLOVES
DILL	CORIANDER
FLAT-LEAF PARSLEY	CUMIN
MINT	FENNEL SEEDS
OREGANO	NUTMEG
ROSEMARY	OREGANO
SAGE	PAPRIKA
TARRAGON	PEPPER (freshly ground white and black)
THYME	SAFFRON
	SUMAC

Synonymous with Greek baking are two distinct aromatic spices: mahlepi and mastiha, which you'll find in my No-knead Easter Tsoureki (page 28) and New Year's Day Cake (page 182). Mahlepi is made from the ground seeds of the mahaleb cherry, and mastiha is a crystal resin derived from the mastic tree exclusive to the Greek island of Chios. Both can be found at European delis and gourmet grocers.

MEAT & SEAFOOD

When it comes to animal proteins, the Mediterranean diet promotes organic, grass-fed meat that is free of pesticides and chemicals. Organic chicken is juicier and more flavoursome than non-organic options, and grass-fed red meat is higher in vitamins and healthy fats like omega 3 than grain-fed meat.

When buying seafood, wild caught is the healthier option. It has fewer toxins and chemicals because the fish feed on a diet of smaller fish and algae in their natural habitat. Overall, organic and wild-caught proteins are more expensive, but they taste far superior and are better for you.

NUTS & SEEDS

Nuts and seeds have featured heavily in the Mediterranean diet since ancient times. They are an integral part of both sweet and savoury dishes, with their high-protein content making them satiating as well as delicious. The most commonly used nuts and seeds are walnuts, pistachios, almonds, pine nuts and sesame seeds. Syrupy sweets like Loukoumades (page 168) and baklava (page 175) are always generously decorated with nuts for added texture and flavour.

OILS, FATS & VINEGARS

EXTRA-VIRGIN OLIVE OIL (EVOO)
EVOO forms the foundation of Mediterranean cooking. Extra virgin is the first cold-pressed oil derived from the olive, retaining the most health benefits, as well as an intense olive flavour. Contrary to what you may have heard, you can fry with a good-quality EVOO – just make sure you don't overheat the pan. EVOO has a smoke point of 200–210°C, which is above the 180°C required for deep-frying. Light EVOO is further refined so it has a mild, delicate flavour and is more suited to baking or mayonnaise when you don't want an overt olive taste.

NATURAL GREEK YOGHURT
Thicker and creamier than regular yoghurt, natural Greek yoghurt has had the whey strained from it. If your yoghurt is not thick enough, you can strain it in a muslin cloth for a few hours for the creamy texture that is required to make dips like Tzatziki (page 208).

ORGANIC BUTTER
In the Mediterranean butter is primarily used in baking for cakes and biscuits. Organic butter has a creamier texture and smoother flavour than other varieties; always choose the best-quality butter you can afford. I prefer to use unsalted organic butter so I can control the salt content.

ORGANIC EGGS
Fresh organic eggs not only taste better than non-organic eggs, they also contain higher amounts of omega 3 fatty acids and vitamins A and E. Organic eggs are also free of harmful added hormones and antibiotics. I use large organic eggs (55 g) in my recipes.

TAHINI
Made from ground sesame seeds, tahini is a staple across the Middle East. It is one of the hardest-working ingredients in a Mediterranean pantry and can be used for anything from dips to salad dressings and cakes and cookies. Tahini is a fantastic vegan substitute when you want to add creaminess to a dish without any dairy. Good-quality tahini is runny and smooth (not thick and claggy!); you should be able to pour it out of your jar.

VINEGARS
The most commonly used vinegars in Mediterranean cooking are white wine, red wine, balsamic and sherry vinegar. For a classic Mediterranean salad dressing, whisk together one part vinegar with three parts extra-virgin olive oil, along with a pinch of sea salt flakes and freshly ground black pepper (the ratio can be adjusted slightly to suit personal taste).

PULSES & LEGUMES

Pulses and legumes form the basis of many Mediterranean dishes, so it is important to have a wide variety stocked in your pantry. Pulses are the dried edible seeds from a legume plant and include lentils, peas (yellow split peas) and beans (chickpeas, kidney beans and cannellini beans). The dried beans are far superior in taste and texture to canned varieties, so get into the habit of planning your meal the night before to allow time to soak them in water overnight. Here is a list of those most commonly used:

BLACK-EYE PEAS	MAVROMATAKIA (PAGE 44)
CANNELLINI BEANS	FASOLADA (PAGE 66)
CHICKPEAS	HUMMUS (PAGE 210)
FAVA BEANS	TA'AMEYA (PAGE 70)
LENTILS	MEJADRA (PAGE 69)
YELLOW SPLIT PEAS	FAVA (PAGE 210)

Fresh legumes include fresh peas (Tomato-braised Peas and Vegetables, page 72), green beans, snow peas and sugar snap peas.

SWEETENERS

MEDJOOL DATES
Often referred to as nature's caramel, medjool dates have a soft chewy texture and a richer taste than regular dates, which are smaller, firmer and less flavoursome. Because medjool dates are a fresh fruit you'll find them with the fresh produce rather than in the dried fruit section of the supermarket or grocer. They are high in potassium, magnesium, iron and other minerals and vitamins.

RAW HONEY
Unprocessed and not heat treated, raw honey is a pure, full-bodied honey that retains beneficial antioxidant and nutritional properties, such as vitamin B6, zinc and potassium. Pasteurisation and heating reduce honey's antifungal and antibacterial benefits, so it is worth paying a little extra for a raw variety.

SUGAR
Caster sugar is used in baking for occasional treats. The Mediterranean diet is more of a lifestyle than a strict diet plan, so there is no need to feel guilty about dunking biscotti in your afternoon coffee.

Icing sugar mixture combines icing sugar with cornflour to stop the sugar from hardening, so you have a soft, luscious finish (Olive Oil Chocolate Cake with Olive Oil Icing, page 192). Check the label to ensure there is no wheat starch added to the mixture.

Pure icing sugar sets quickly and firmly and is ideal for royal icing and glazes (Fluffy Lemon, Ricotta and Blueberry Loaf, page 186).

Ten tips to transition to a gluten-free Mediterranean diet

1. Swap butter for extra-virgin olive oil

Extra-virgin olive oil is the primary fat source in the Mediterranean diet and is a much healthier option than butter. Extra-virgin olive oil is lower in saturated fat, contains large amounts of antioxidants as well as oleocanthal, a strong anti-inflammatory compound that gives the oil its peppery taste. Save butter for occasional baked treats and desserts.

2. Eat more plants

Vegan and vegetarian dishes feature heavily in Mediterranean cuisine, relying on an abundance of seasonal fresh fruits and vegetables, legumes, pulses, nuts and seeds. The large consumption of local plant foods is a key reason the Mediterranean diet has been repeatedly proven as the healthiest in the world. The high ratio of antioxidant-rich and anti-inflammatory plant foods plays a significant role in fighting chronic diseases and improving heart health, hence the longevity of Ikarians and Sardinians in the 'Blue Zones'. Fruits and vegetables should make up the bulk of your meals.

3. Replace bulgur wheat and couscous with quinoa

Quinoa seeds are light and fluffy when cooked, so they are a fantastic nutrient-dense replacement for couscous to soak up sauces in slow-cooked stews. Blitz warm quinoa seeds to a pliable paste and you can create crispy shells for kibbeh and Koupes (page 160) to replace a bulgur wheat casing. Quinoa is also a great replacement for bulgur wheat in tabbouleh (page 47), providing a lighter and more delicate texture in this vibrant salad.

4. Learn to cook with polenta

Polenta is so much more than just a delicious creamy replacement for rice and potatoes. In a fraction of the time it takes to make traditional pastry, you can whip up an easy crispy polenta pie crust by simply mixing it with some water and olive oil. Its similar gritty texture also makes polenta a great replacement for semolina in syrupy cakes. You might also like to try your hand at making a rustic polenta cornbread (page 27), just as the Mediterraneans have done since ancient times.

5. Keep it simple

Mediterranean cooking is all about simplicity. Forget heavy creamy salad dressings and overly adorned cakes. To let good-quality seasonal produce shine, generally all that is required is a drizzle of olive oil, a squeeze of lemon juice and a pinch of sea salt flakes. In ancient times, peasants survived on inexpensive, unprocessed nutrient-dense food and that's still the healthiest approach today.

6. Eat less red meat and more seafood

Limit consumption of red meat to one or two times per week and choose organic grass-fed meat where possible. Lean chicken is a healthier option if you want to eat meat more frequently. Teach yourself creative new seafood recipes so you can move beyond grilled fish for express mid-week meals. Try poaching firm white fillets in tasty broths and winter seafood stews, or pickling octopus for a salad, or baking whole snapper to feed the family. Seafood contains high doses of omega 3 fatty acids, which reduce inflammation and can improve cholesterol levels.

7. Enjoy artisanal cheeses and yoghurt in moderation

Goat's and sheep's milk cheeses are the most popular cheeses in the Mediterranean, and are a healthier lower-fat option when compared to aged cow's milk cheeses like cheddar. Greek feta is quite rich in flavour, so you need only a small quantity to satisfy your cheese craving. A scattering of sharp pecorino over pasta is all you need for an umami hit.

8. Indulge in an occasional sweet treat with friends

Mediterraneans love their sweets, but they are mostly enjoyed with visitors or as a celebratory treat to foster social connections. Loukoumades (page 168) are freshly cooked at the end of a meal to feed crowds at a party, and platters of biscuits are exchanged during religious periods to mark special festivities. There are no strict rules here; feel free to dunk your biscotti or koulouri in your black coffee as long as everything else is kept in balance.

9. Snack on nuts and olives

To satisfy salty snack cravings, reach for a handful of nuts or olives instead of processed packaged foods. Nuts and olives are a good source of protein, healthy monounsaturated fats, antioxidants, vitamins and minerals.

10. Sip a little wine

In the Mediterranean, wine is generally consumed in small amounts to accompany a meal. Excessive drinking without food is uncommon. A glass of red wine is there to be savoured and to enhance the flavour of the food, quite often as a communal shared experience with family and friends. Avoid all soft drinks.

BREADS &

PIES

Focaccia

500 g Italian gluten-free bread flour (see Note)

7 g sachet dried yeast

3 teaspoons sea salt flakes, plus extra for sprinkling

3 tablespoons extra-virgin olive oil, plus extra for brushing and drizzling

DF, GF, VG | SERVES 12

Forget kneading and overcomplicated steps, this gluten-free version of the iconic Italian bread comes together in a flash – and the results are incredible: a perfectly crisp golden top, crunchy olive oil base and light and fluffy centre. The most challenging part is waiting an hour for the dough to puff up, that's as difficult as it gets. It is critical to use an Italian gluten-free bread flour for this recipe to achieve the correct results. The added starches in the gluten-free bread flour provide the extra stretch that enables the dough to rise.

Brush a baking tray (roughly 30 cm × 23 cm) generously with olive oil.

Place the flour, yeast and salt in the bowl of an electric mixer fitted with the paddle attachment and mix on low speed to combine. Add 450 ml of warm water and the olive oil and mix to form a wet batter.

Spoon the batter onto the prepared tray and spread out with the back of an oiled spoon to completely cover the base. Drizzle some extra oil over the batter, use your fingers to create dimples over the top, then cover with plastic wrap and rest in a warm spot for 1 hour.

Preheat the oven to 220°C (fan-forced).

Remove the plastic wrap and sprinkle some extra salt over the top. Bake for 35–40 minutes or until golden. So the crust remains crispy, immediately transfer the focaccia to a wire rack to cool.

VARIATIONS

— Olive & Rosemary: prior to resting the dough, press 155 g (1 cup) pitted kalamata olives into the dough and sprinkle on 1 tablespoon coarsely chopped rosemary leaves. Drizzle some extra oil over the dough, then cover in plastic wrap.

— Pugliese: prior to resting the dough, press 150 g halved cherry tomatoes into the dough and sprinkle with 1 teaspoon dried oregano. Drizzle some extra oil over the dough, then cover in plastic wrap. Just before baking, sprinkle on some extra salt.

— Gluten-free Dinner Rolls: spoon the batter into a greased 12-hole large muffin tin. Cover with plastic wrap, rest for 1 hour, then bake for 20–25 minutes or until the rolls are golden.

NOTE

— You can find Italian gluten-free bread flour at European delis and gourmet grocers.

Cypriot Haloumi Bread

2 small handfuls of sesame and/or nigella seeds, for sprinkling

4 eggs, at room temperature

250 ml (1 cup) light olive oil

125 ml (½ cup) milk

300 g haloumi, grated

200 g provolone picante, grated

260 g (2 cups) gluten-free self-raising flour, sifted

large handful of mint leaves, finely chopped

pinch of sea salt flakes and freshly ground white pepper

GF, V | **SERVES 10**

Haloumi bread was one of the first breads I ever baked when I was a kid. It is so easy to whip up in one bowl, that even 12-year-old me could master it. My Cypriot neighbours taught me this recipe and passed on their secret tip for the best-ever haloumi bread – two cheeses, not one. Haloumi for salty firmness and provolone picante for a sharp oozy cheesiness with stretch and extra flavour. Feta also works very well as the second cheese. Some recipes call for dried mint, but I find the flavour of fresh mint more vibrant and refreshing. Optional additions include a handful of sultanas for little pops of sweetness, juicy pitted kalamata olives or caramelised onions.

Preheat the oven to 180°C (fan-forced). Grease a 20 cm bundt tin, sprinkle in a small handful of sesame and/or nigella seeds and tilt the tin to cover the base and sides.

In a large bowl, whisk together the eggs, olive oil and milk. Add the cheeses, flour, mint, salt and white pepper and whisk to combine until you have a thick, wet batter.

Spoon the batter into the prepared tin and sprinkle the remaining seeds over the top. Bake for 40 minutes or until the bread is golden. Cool in the tin for 1 hour, then turn out and slice to serve. Store in an airtight container at room temperature up to 3 days.

Pita Bread

½ teaspoon caster sugar

1 teaspoon dried yeast

195 g (1½ cups) gluten-free plain flour

1 teaspoon sea salt flakes

1 tablespoon extra-virgin olive oil, plus extra for drizzling

DF, GF, VG | **MAKES 4**

Traditionally, the way to start a meal at any Greek taverna is with soft warm pita bread accompanied by a medley of dips. My favourites are garlicky Tzatziki (page 208), because you can smear it on literally anything; salty Taramasalata (page 209), for its light and fluffy texture; Fava (page 210), for its distinctive creaminess; and Melitzanosalata (page 211), for its smoky eggplant notes. When dining out, I'm often served veggie sticks as a bread substitute, but what I really want is a soft pliable gluten-free bread to scoop up my dip like everyone else. Here is my easy recipe for pita, so you never have to miss out again.

Place the caster sugar, yeast and 180 ml (¾ cup) of lukewarm water in a jug and whisk to combine. Leave to stand for 10–15 minutes or until the mixture foams.

Place the flour in the bowl of an electric mixer fitted with the dough hook attachment and crush in the salt flakes with your fingers. Pour in the yeast mixture and olive oil and mix for about 1 minute to form a ball.

Transfer the dough to a large, greased bowl, cover with plastic wrap and rest in a warm spot for 1 hour or until the dough has doubled in size. (If you are making the dough ahead of time, it will keep in the fridge for up to 3 days.)

Divide the dough into four even portions and roll into balls. Working with one ball at a time, drizzle over a little olive oil and massage to coat. Place the dough between two sheets of baking paper and roll out to form a thin 20 cm round.

Heat a cast-iron frying pan over high heat and drizzle in a little olive oil. Remove the top layer of baking paper from the dough, then flip the round into the hot pan and peel away the remaining baking paper. Cook for 2–3 minutes on each side or until golden and puffy. Remove the bread from the pan and cover with a tea towel to keep warm while you cook the rest.

Bobota
Village Cornbread

150 g (1 cup) polenta

130 g (1 cup) gluten-free
self-raising flour

1 teaspoon sea salt flakes

¼ teaspoon bicarbonate of soda

250 g canned creamed corn

80 ml (⅓ cup) light olive oil

125 ml (½ cup) milk (or dairy-free
milk of your choice)

2 eggs

1 tablespoon honey

DFO, GF, V | SERVES 8–10

Bobota is a rustic cornbread, with many regional variations, that is consumed throughout Greece. Historically, it was considered 'poor man's food' because it was a cheap, nutrient-dense meal that peasants could rely on to get them through difficult times. Growing up, I loved eating warm bobota smeared with butter and occasionally drizzled with honey for breakfast. This no-fuss recipe is for a basic bobota. From here, you can add your favourite inclusions to create a savoury cheese and herb version or a sweet cornbread with raisins and orange zest.

Preheat the oven to 180°C (fan-forced). Generously grease a 26 cm cast-iron frying pan and place in the oven for 5 minutes to heat up (this helps create a crispy crust on your bread).

Meanwhile, place the polenta, flour, salt and bicarbonate of soda in a large bowl and mix to combine. Add the creamed corn, olive oil, milk, eggs and honey and mix to form a smooth, wet batter.

Remove the hot pan from the oven, pour in the batter and smooth the top with a spatula. Bake for 25 minutes or until golden. So the base remains crispy, immediately turn out the cornbread onto a wire rack. Cool slightly, then slice and serve warm. Store in an airtight container at room temperature up to 3 days.

VARIATIONS

— Feta & Thyme: add 200 g crumbled Greek feta and 1 tablespoon thyme leaves to your batter.

— Raisin & Orange: add 40 g (⅓ cup) raisins, 1 teaspoon finely grated orange zest and 1 teaspoon ground cinnamon to your batter.

— Syrupy Bobota: combine 175 g (½ cup) honey, 250 ml (1 cup) of water and a 5 cm orange peel strip in a small saucepan. Simmer for 5 minutes to thicken. Pour the cooled syrup over the just-cooked bobota (prick the surface with a toothpick first – this helps the syrup soak into the bobota). Cool, then serve.

No-knead Easter Tsoureki

250 ml (1 cup) lukewarm milk

2 x 7 g sachets dried yeast

230 g (1 cup) caster sugar

390 g (3 cups) gluten-free plain flour

2 teaspoons gluten-free baking powder

1 teaspoon mahlepi (see Notes)

½ teaspoon ground mastiha (see Notes)

1 teaspoon finely grated orange zest

pinch of sea salt flakes

50 g butter, melted, plus 1 tablespoon extra, for drizzling

1 teaspoon vanilla extract

3 eggs, lightly whisked, at room temperature

2 tablespoons flaked almonds

3 red eggs (optional) (see Notes)

DFO, GF, V | SERVES 12

Tsoureki is a traditional Greek Easter sweet bread, similar to brioche. Traditionally, tsoureki is plaited; however, a gluten-free tsoureki dough is wetter and softer than regular dough, so it is difficult to plait without adding an excessive amount of flour. The solution? Treat your yeasted dough like a thick, wet cake batter and in a fraction of the time it takes to cook a traditional tsoureki you will have a super light and fluffy no-knead bread infused with stunning aroma and flavour. Representing the blood of Christ, the red eggs are an optional but beautiful addition.

Grease a 23 cm bundt tin (or a 23 cm round cake tin).

Place the milk, yeast and half the caster sugar in a small bowl and stir to combine. Rest for 15 minutes until the yeast foams.

Combine the flour and the remaining sugar with the baking powder, mahlepi, mastiha, orange zest and salt in a large bowl and mix well. Pour in the yeasty milk mixture, melted butter, vanilla extract and egg and stir to form a thick, wet batter. Spoon the batter into the prepared tin. Spread out and smooth the top with a spatula, then sprinkle on the flaked almonds. Cover with plastic wrap and rest in a warm spot for about an hour until the dough almost doubles in size.

Preheat the oven to 180°C (fan-forced).

Drizzle the extra melted butter over the dough and arrange the red eggs on top (if using). Bake for 25 minutes or until golden. Rest for an hour in the tin before slicing. Store in an airtight container at room temperature for up to 3 days.

VARIATIONS

— For a dairy-free version, replace the butter with light olive oil and the milk with your favourite dairy-free milk, such as almond or macadamia milk.

— You can replace the flaked almonds with sesame seeds, or omit.

NOTES

— How to make red eggs: place 500 ml (2 cups) of water, 3 tablespoons white vinegar and 10 g powdered red food dye in a small saucepan and bring to a simmer over medium–low heat. Gently lower the eggs into the water and simmer for 8 minutes or until the desired colour is achieved. Remove the eggs and cool on a plate, then polish with an oiled cloth for a shiny finish. Note that after being baked into the tsoureki, the red eggs are generally considered purely decorative, though they can be eaten within 2 hours at room temperature.

— Mahlepi, mastiha and red food dye can be found at European delis.

Gozleme

...urkish gozleme can be easily whipped up
...e perfect after-school snack. The dough
...d while it's resting, you can quickly
...e a spiced lamb mince filling when
...d feta, but you can get as creative
...me – the flatter the parcel the
...t frying pan.

...bowl of an electric mixer fitted
...d 125 ml (½ cup) of warm water and
...nute to form a smooth dough. If the mixture
...ore water and mix again. Set the dough aside to rest,
...e you make the filling.

...ke the filling, heat the olive oil in a frying pan over medium heat.
Add the onion and salt and cook for 5 minutes to soften. Stir in the garlic,
paprika, cumin and black pepper and cook for 30 seconds. Add the lamb
and cook, breaking up any chunks with a wooden spoon, for 3 minutes
or until browned. Add the spinach, stir and cook for 1 minute to wilt.
Remove from the heat and set aside.

Divide the dough into six balls. Working with one ball at a time, roll out the
dough between two sheets of baking paper to form a paper-thin rectangle
about 20 cm × 30 cm in size. Scatter 3 tablespoons of the lamb and spinach
filling in the centre, leaving a clear border of roughly 8 cm around the edges.
Fold the dough over the filling to enclose. Cover with baking paper and very
gently roll out again to flatten and thin out the gozleme. Repeat with the
remaining dough and filling.

Place a heavy-based frying pan over high heat and allow it to heat up.
Drizzle 1 tablespoon of olive oil into the very hot pan and cook the gozleme,
one at a time, adding more oil as needed, for 2–3 minutes on each side until
golden and crispy. Serve with lemon wedges.

...pped

...rika

...poon ground cumin

pinch of freshly ground
black pepper

250 g lamb mince

large handful of baby
spinach leaves

DFO, GF | SERVES 6

FILLING VARIATIONS

—Spinach & Feta: combine 135 g (3 cups) baby spinach, 3 sliced spring
  onions and 200 g crumbled feta.

—Potato & Cheese: combine 460 g (2 cups) mashed potato, 150 g grated
  mozzarella, a handful of finely chopped flat-leaf parsley leaves,
  ½ teaspoon paprika and salt and pepper.

Kalitsounia
My Mum's Ricotta Pies

500 g fresh ricotta, well drained

200 g Greek feta, crumbled

1 egg

3 tablespoons finely chopped mint leaves

1 teaspoon sea salt flakes

1 x quantity Olive Oil Pastry (page 206)

extra-virgin olive oil, for spraying

sesame seeds, for sprinkling

GF, V | MAKES 16

Kalitsounia are small ricotta pies from my mother's island of Crete. Each region in Crete has its own way of preparing them. They are enjoyed baked, fried, savoury or sweet with a drizzle of warm honey or dusting of cinnamon sugar. My mother has always preferred to bake her ricotta and mint kalitsounia, as it is the healthier way to cook them; and because the baked version stores well, she would often pack them in my school lunchbox for the next few days. You can shape the dough into frilly discs, like she does, or completely enclose the ricotta in pastry to form little crescents or squares.

Preheat the oven to 200°C (fan-forced). Line a baking tray with baking paper.

Combine the ricotta, feta, egg, mint and salt in a bowl.

Divide the olive oil pastry into four portions. Working with one portion at a time, carefully roll out the pastry between two sheets of baking paper until it is paper thin (try not to break it). Cut out four pastry rounds with an 11 cm cutter. Spoon 2 tablespoons of the filling into the centre of each round and smooth out the filling, leaving a 1 cm border around the edge. Fold the pastry edge around the filling, pinching as you go to create a pleated border. Repeat with the remaining dough and filling until you have 16 pies.

Transfer the pies to the prepared tray, spray the surface with olive oil and sprinkle over some sesame seeds. Bake for 20 minutes or until the pies are crispy and golden. Serve warm. Store in an airtight container in the fridge up to 3 days and reheat prior to serving if you wish.

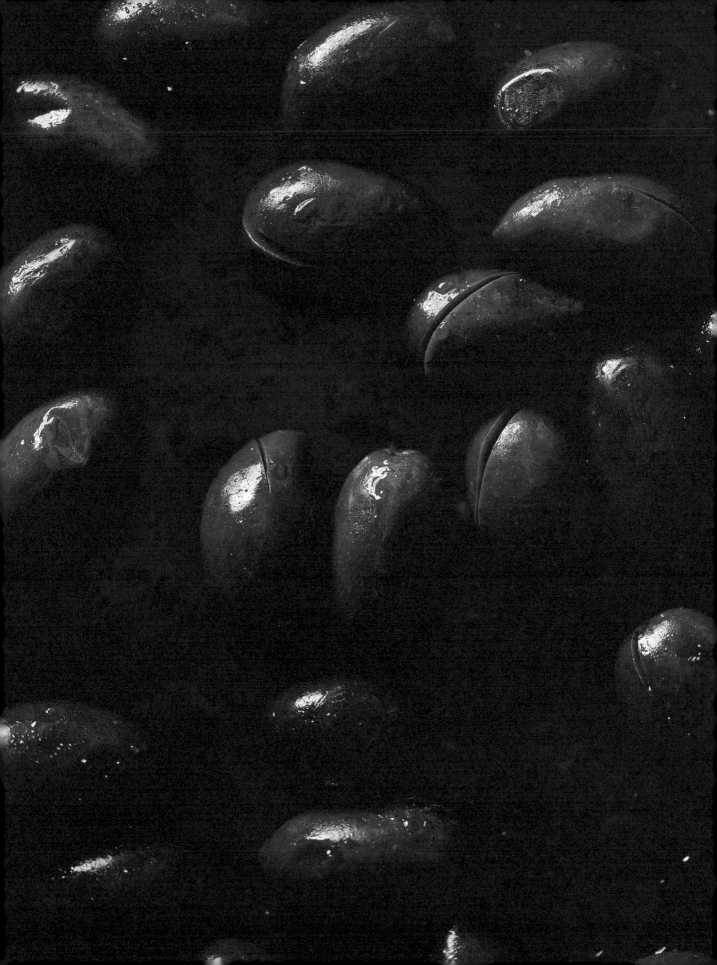

Plastos
Polenta-crusted Spanakopita

light olive oil, for brushing and spraying

POLENTA CRUST

400 g polenta

200 ml extra-virgin olive oil

2 teaspoons sea salt flakes

pinch of freshly ground black pepper

SPINACH FILLING

1 bunch of English spinach, trimmed, leaves finely sliced

6 spring onions, finely sliced

handful of dill fronds, finely chopped

handful of mint leaves, finely chopped

300 g fresh ricotta, drained

200 g Greek feta, crumbled

1 egg

generous pinch of freshly ground black pepper

pinch of sea salt flakes

DFO, GF, V | **SERVES 12**

Plastos is a cheese and spinach pie originating from Thessaly in Northern Greece, where corn plantations are abundant. Unlike traditional spanakopita, which is encased in pastry, plastos has a polenta crust that is much quicker to make and is equally delicious. You simply sandwich the spinach and cheese filling between thin layers of polenta mixture and what results is a delicious savoury pie with a golden, crunchy, no-fuss crust. Feel free to use a variety of mixed leafy greens – silverbeet works well.

Preheat the oven to 200°C (fan-forced). Generously brush a shallow baking tray (30 cm × 25 cm × 2 cm) with olive oil.

Combine the polenta crust ingredients in a large bowl, add 150 ml of warm water and thoroughly mix with your hands until the mixture resembles wet sand. Let the mixture rest for 10 minutes to firm up.

Meanwhile, combine the spinach filling ingredients in a separate large bowl. Mix with your hands, firmly squeezing the spinach so it wilts and softens.

Transfer half the crust mixture to the prepared tray and firmly press it into the base and sides to form a thin layer. (The polenta crust should be paper thin; you can place a sheet of baking paper on top and use a spatula to help spread it.)

Spoon the filling over the polenta base and firmly smooth it out.

Add 80 ml (⅓ cup) of water to the remaining crust mixture in the bowl and mix with your hands until it resembles very wet sand. Spread the mixture over the filling, using a spatula to smooth it out – don't worry if there are tiny gaps on the surface, the pie will still form a firm top crust when baked. Spray the surface with olive oil and bake for 50–60 minutes or until the plastos is golden and crunchy on top. Rest for 15 minutes on the tray, then slice and serve. Store in an airtight container in the fridge up to 3 days and reheat prior to serving if you wish.

VARIATION

— For a dairy-free option, omit the cheese in the filling.

Batzina
Crustless Zucchini Pie

600 g zucchini, coarsely grated

sea salt flakes and freshly ground white pepper

4 eggs

large handful of mint leaves, finely chopped

small handful of dill fronds, finely chopped

4 spring onions, finely sliced

200 g Greek feta, crumbled

finely grated zest of 1 small lemon

2 tablespoons olive oil, plus extra for drizzling

200 g gluten-free self-raising flour

80 g (½ cup) sesame seeds, for sprinkling

GF, V | **SERVES 8**

Batzina is a crustless pie originating from Epirus and Thessaly in Northern Greece. Greeks refer to it as the 'lazy pie' because you don't need to worry about prepping the dough – it can be thrown together quickly and easily. The grated zucchini, creamy feta and eggs make the pie incredibly moist, with the dill and mint adding freshness and flavour. It is important to get the thickness of your pie right. You don't want it too thick, so use the pan size specified to ensure a gorgeous golden crust and perfectly set filling.

Preheat the oven to 180°C (fan-forced). Grease a 25 cm × 30 cm baking tray.

Toss the grated zucchini with a pinch of salt, place in a colander and set aside for 20 minutes. Squeeze out the excess moisture from the zucchini.

Whisk the eggs in a large bowl. Add the zucchini, mint, dill, spring onion, feta, lemon zest, olive oil and a pinch of salt and white pepper, and mix to combine. Add the flour and mix with a wooden spoon until you have a thick batter.

Sprinkle half the sesame seeds over the base of the prepared tray, then spoon in the batter and spread out evenly. Drizzle with olive oil (or use oil spray if you prefer) and sprinkle on the remaining sesame seeds. Bake for 45 minutes or until the pie is golden. Cool slightly and serve warm. Store in an airtight container in the fridge up to 3 days and reheat prior to serving if you wish.

SAL
ADS

Radicchio, Blistered Grape & Goat's Cheese Salad

200 g seedless red grapes

2 tablespoons sesame seeds

1 small radicchio (about 250 g), quartered and leaves separated

1 baby cos lettuce (about 150 g), leaves separated

100 g soft goat's cheese, torn

handful of chives, finely chopped

SIMPLE SALAD DRESSING

100 ml extra-virgin olive oil

2 tablespoons sherry vinegar

2 teaspoons raw honey

1 banana shallot, finely chopped

pinch of sea salt flakes and freshly ground black pepper

DFO, GF, V | SERVES 4–6

When grapes sit under a hot grill they blister and caramelise to become extra juicy and jammy – a shortcut way of turning a simple salad into something magical. The sweetness of the blistered grapes combined with the sherry vinegar and honey dressing mellow the sharpness of the radicchio in this stunning salad. A scattering of salty, creamy goat's cheese and crunchy toasted sesame seeds adds another layer of contrasting textures.

Preheat the oven grill to high.

Spread the grapes in a single layer over a small baking tray and place under the hot grill for 8 minutes until softened. Remove the tray, gently shake to turn the grapes, then sprinkle on the sesame seeds. Grill for another 6 minutes or until the sesame seeds are toasted and the grapes have blistered.

Layer the radicchio and lettuce leaves on a large serving platter. Scatter on the goat's cheese and chives.

Whisk together the dressing ingredients, then spoon over the salad. Scatter on the warm blistered grapes and toasted sesame seeds and serve immediately.

VARIATION
—For a dairy-free option, you can replace the cheese with avocado chunks for creaminess.

Mavromatakia
Black-eye Pea Salad

250 g dried black-eye peas

8 cherry tomatoes, halved

1 large carrot, coarsely grated

½ red capsicum, finely sliced

5 spring onions, finely sliced

handful of mint leaves,
finely chopped

handful of dill fronds,
finely chopped

handful of flat-leaf parsley leaves,
finely chopped

HONEY–MUSTARD DRESSING

100 ml extra-virgin olive oil

3 tablespoons red wine vinegar

1 teaspoon honey

1 teaspoon dijon mustard

1 small garlic clove, crushed

pinch of sea salt flakes and
freshly ground black pepper

DF, GF, VGO | SERVES 6–8

Black-eye peas (also called black-eye beans) are a staple ingredient in the North Aegean islands of Greece. They commonly feature in braised vegan stews and are delicious mixed with wild greens. These small nutrient-dense peas ('mavro' meaning black and 'matakia' meaning eye) are bursting with protein, fibre and antioxidants, and are a fantastic base for this healthy and vibrant salad. This is quite a versatile recipe that comes together with a bright and zesty honey vinaigrette, so feel free to add other chopped vegetables.

Place the black-eye peas in a saucepan and cover with plenty of cold water. Place over medium heat and bring to the boil. Reduce the heat to low and simmer for 25 minutes until the peas are al dente. (Be careful not to overcook them or they will quickly turn mushy.) Drain and rinse under cold water. Set aside to allow the peas to cool completely.

Whisk together the honey–mustard dressing ingredients in a large bowl. Add the remaining salad ingredients and peas and gently toss to combine. Transfer the salad to a platter and serve.

VARIATION
— For a vegan option, replace the honey with maple syrup.

Tabbouleh with Quinoa

100 g (½ cup) cooked and cooled white quinoa

1 bunch of flat-leaf parsley, leaves picked and finely chopped

large handful of mint leaves, finely chopped

5 spring onions, finely sliced

3 tomatoes, diced

1 large Lebanese cucumber, diced

3 tablespoons extra-virgin olive oil

3 tablespoons freshly squeezed lemon juice

2 teaspoons sea salt flakes

¼ teaspoon freshly ground black pepper

DF, GF, VG | SERVES 6

Quinoa is a fantastic gluten-free substitute for bulgur wheat in this stunning Lebanese salad. While bulgur and quinoa may taste very similar in a salad mix, quinoa is lighter in texture and more nutrient dense as it is a complete protein – containing all nine essential amino acids – and is high in fibre and antioxidants. Win win! Remember to rinse and cook your quinoa first and allow it to cool completely before mixing it with your veggies and herbs (you don't want them to go soggy). This refreshing, healthy vegan salad is the perfect addition to any Mediterranean meal.

Place the quinoa, herbs, spring onion, tomato and cucumber in a large bowl and toss to combine. Add the olive oil, lemon juice, salt and pepper and toss again. Taste and adjust the seasoning as required. Serve immediately.

Figs, Prosciutto & Whipped Ricotta

8 figs, halved

5 thin slices of prosciutto, torn

handful of basil leaves

1 tablespoon extra-virgin olive oil

2 teaspoons balsamic vinegar

pinch of freshly ground
black pepper

WHIPPED RICOTTA

400 g fresh ricotta, drained

1 tablespoon honey

pinch of sea salt flakes

DFO, GF | **SERVES 4–6**

When figs are in season – late summer to mid-autumn – I whip up this salad for dinner guests when I need something that tastes delicious and looks impressive. The plump, juicy figs do most of the work. Native to the Mediterranean, this sweet, ancient fruit is the perfect companion to salty prosciutto, whipped airy ricotta, fresh basil and grassy extra-virgin olive oil.

Blitz the whipped ricotta ingredients in a food processor until smooth.

Spoon the whipped ricotta onto a platter and spread out thinly to create a blanket. Scatter on the figs, prosciutto and basil.

Whisk together the olive oil, balsamic vinegar and black pepper. Drizzle the dressing over the salad and serve.

VARIATION
— For a dairy-free version, you can serve your salad without the ricotta blanket – it still tastes spectacular.

NUTRITION NOTE
— Figs are fantastic for digestive health and are a great source of fibre, antioxidants, vitamins and minerals.

Rustic Heirloom Tomato Salad

1 kg ripe heirloom tomatoes
(various colours), cut into 1 cm
thick slices

1 small red onion,
sliced into thin rounds

1 small yellow capsicum,
sliced into thin rounds

handful of baby basil leaves

sea salt flakes and freshly
ground black pepper

extra-virgin olive oil, for drizzling

DF, GF, VG | **SERVES 4–6**

Ask anyone who has travelled to the Mediterranean about the tomatoes, and they will generally respond with 'extraordinary, heaven, nothing compares'. I have found all of this to be true. Contributing factors are the mineral-rich volcanic soil, plentiful sunshine and strong demand by locals for outstanding quality in seasonal produce. They are so flavoursome that they only require the best-quality robust extra-virgin olive oil and sea salt flakes to dress them up. To recreate this rustic salad at home, look for the plumpest, juiciest heirloom tomatoes at your local greengrocer and let the quality of the produce shine.

Arrange the tomato slices on a platter. Top with the onion, capsicum and basil and season with a sprinkling of salt and pepper. Drizzle with olive oil to serve.

Nectarine, Rocket & Buffalo Mozzarella Salad

100 g rocket leaves

3 white or yellow nectarines, cut into wedges

1 tablespoon flaked almonds, toasted

200 g buffalo mozzarella

LEMON–HONEY DRESSING

80 ml (⅓ cup) extra-virgin olive oil

juice of 1 small lemon

1 teaspoon honey

pinch of sea salt flakes and freshly ground black pepper

GF, V | SERVES 4–6

Stone fruits are not only delicious as a stand-alone snack, they are also sensational in summer salads. Juicy ripe peaches, sweet succulent nectarines, tart bright plums – I love them all. You can swap out nectarines for peaches in this salad. The goal is to create a platter of contrasting textures and flavours: sweet fruit, bitter rocket, crunchy almonds and creamy cheese. Quality stone fruit is only in season from summer to early autumn, so if you want to make this salad out of season, try juicy pear slices or papaya as a winter substitute.

Arrange the rocket leaves on a platter. Scatter the nectarine wedges and almonds over the rocket. Tear up the mozzarella with your hands and place on top.

Whisk together the lemon–honey dressing ingredients and drizzle the dressing over the salad. Serve immediately.

Patatosalata
Herbed Potato Salad

1 kg chat potatoes, unpeeled and scrubbed

4 spring onions, finely sliced

handful of flat-leaf parsley leaves, finely chopped

handful of dill fronds, finely chopped

RED WINE VINEGAR DRESSING

125 ml (½ cup) extra-virgin olive oil

3 tablespoons red wine vinegar

2 teaspoons dijon mustard

2 teaspoons sea salt flakes

¼ teaspoon freshly ground white pepper

DF, GF, VG | SERVES 4–6

This recipe was one of the first ways my mum introduced me to herbs as a kid. I heard 'potatoes' and I was all in. Mediterranean salads are all about fresh seasonal produce and the best-quality extra-virgin olive oil, not dairy-loaded creamy dressings. The garden herbs and simple red wine vinegar dressing in this rustic salad don't overwhelm the potatoes; instead, they showcase their gorgeous creaminess.

Place the potatoes in a saucepan and cover with cold salted water. Place over medium–high heat and bring to a simmer, then reduce the heat to low and cook, covered, for 20 minutes or until the potatoes are tender. Drain and cool for 10 minutes.

Meanwhile, whisk the red wine vinegar dressing ingredients together in a bowl large enough to toss your salad in.

Slice the potatoes in half lengthways to create a large surface area to soak up the dressing (you don't need to peel the potatoes; you want a rustic finish).

Add the warm potatoes, spring onion and herbs to the dressing in the bowl and gently toss to combine. Transfer the warm salad to a platter and serve.

Politiki
Cabbage Salad

150 g (2 cups) finely shredded red cabbage (preferably using a mandoline)

150 g (2 cups) finely shredded white cabbage (preferably using a mandoline)

1 large carrot, julienned

1 celery stalk, finely sliced (preferably using a mandoline)

1 small red capsicum, finely sliced (preferably using a mandoline)

large handful of flat-leaf parsley leaves, roughly chopped

VINAIGRETTE

80 ml (⅓ cup) extra-virgin olive oil

2 tablespoons white wine vinegar

1 small garlic clove, finely chopped

1 teaspoon sea salt flakes

pinch of freshly ground black pepper

DF, GF, VG | **SERVES 4–6**

'Politiki' means 'of the city'. The city in this context is Constantinople (now Istanbul), and that's where this vibrant salad originates. Typically prepared in winter, the salad base of crispy shredded cabbage is mixed with a kaleidoscope of crunchy vegetables and bathed in a white wine vinaigrette. This salad is all about texture, so be careful not to overdress it – my pet peeve is soggy, limp leaves drowning in dressing; you want a salad with stunning crunch.

Combine all the salad ingredients in a bowl.

Whisk together the vinaigrette ingredients, then pour the dressing over the salad. Toss to combine, taste and adjust the seasoning as required. Serve immediately.

Cannellini Bean & Kalamata Olive Salad

250 g dried cannellini beans, soaked overnight in water (see Note)

2 fresh bay leaves

sea salt flakes

1 celery stalk, diced, leaves reserved and roughly chopped

1 small red onion, finely diced

handful of flat-leaf parsley leaves, finely chopped

handful of mint leaves, finely chopped

10 kalamata olives, pitted and torn

VINEGAR DRESSING

125 ml (½ cup) extra-virgin olive oil

3 tablespoons red wine vinegar

1 garlic clove, finely chopped

pinch of freshly ground black pepper

DF, GF, VG | SERVES 4–6

Cannellini beans are the perfect blank canvas for any salad. They soak up dressings beautifully and their creaminess provides the perfect contrast to crisp herbs and veggies. Throw in a scattering of salty kalamata olives and you have a delicious healthy salad that tastes even better the next day. You can replace the cannellini beans with larger butter beans if you prefer, just simmer for a little longer.

Drain and rinse the cannellini beans and place them in a saucepan with the bay leaves and plenty of water. Bring to the boil, reduce the heat to low, then simmer for 20 minutes. Add a good pinch of salt and simmer for a further 20 minutes or until the beans are just tender. Drain, discard the bay leaves, and set the beans aside for 15 minutes to cool.

Meanwhile, place the vinegar dressing ingredients and a pinch of salt in a large bowl and whisk to combine.

Add the beans, celery, onion, parsley, mint and olives to the bowl and gently toss. Transfer the salad to a serving bowl, then scatter on the reserved celery leaves and serve.

NOTE

— You can use canned cannellini beans if you don't have time to soak and cook them, but the flavour and texture of the dried beans will always be superior.

LEGUMES, PULSES

VEGE T

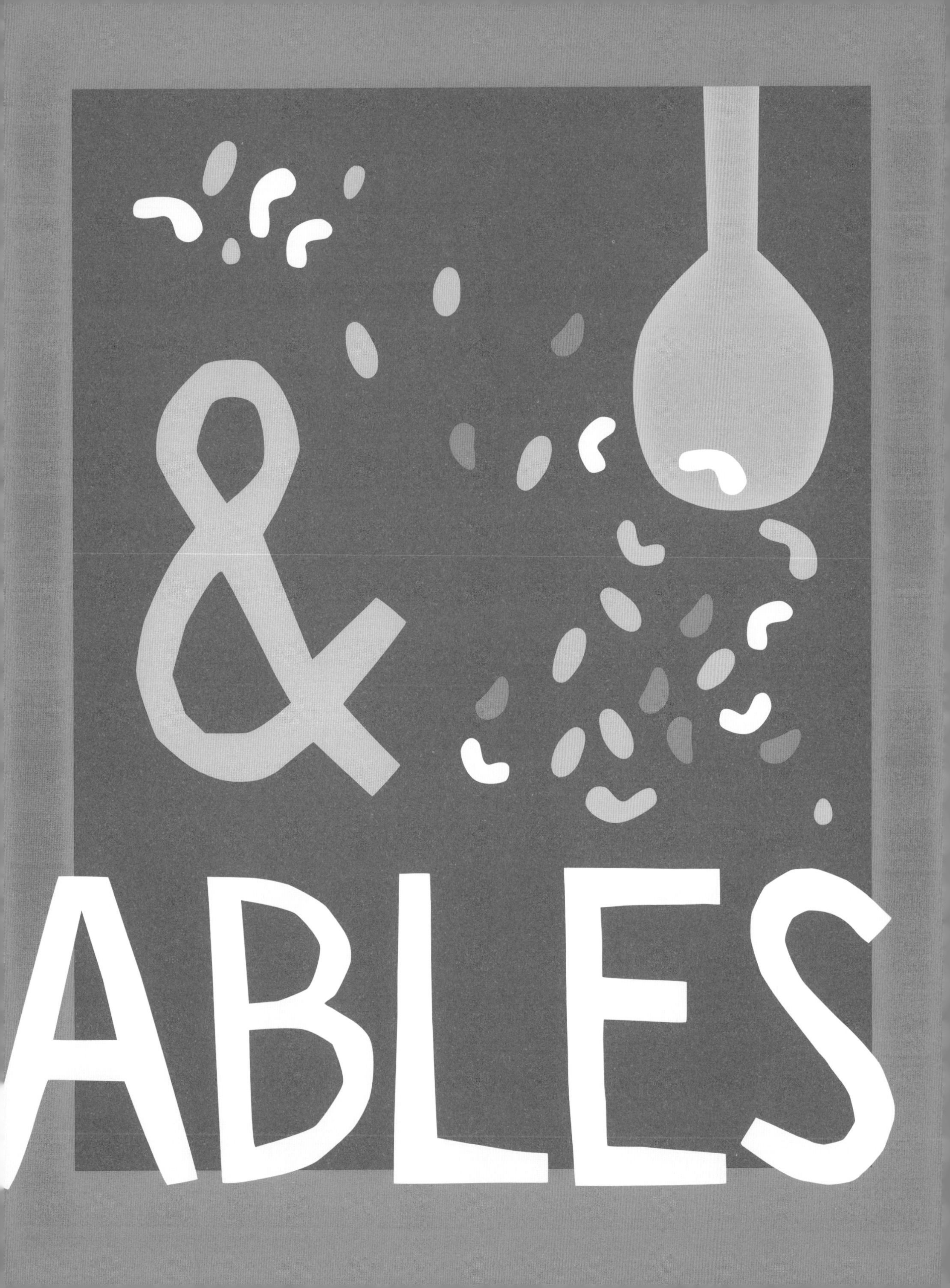
&
ABLES

Revithosoupa
Chickpea Soup

300 g dried chickpeas,
soaked overnight in water

125 ml (½ cup) extra-virgin olive oil,
plus extra for drizzling

1 large onion, finely chopped

2 celery stalks, finely chopped

2 carrots, finely chopped

sea salt flakes and freshly ground
black pepper

2 garlic cloves, finely chopped

2 fresh bay leaves

1 tablespoon thyme leaves

juice of 1 large lemon

handful of flat-leaf parsley leaves
or dill fronds, finely chopped

DF, GF, VG | SERVES 4–6

This is one of those soups I hated as a kid but love as an adult.
It is easy and inexpensive as it requires only dried chickpeas and
a handful of fresh vegetables for a hearty, wholesome and incredibly
flavoursome meal. The key to getting a luscious, creamy texture is
to blitz a few cups of the cooked soup in a food processor at the
end of simmering, then return the puree to the soup. Perfect for
a winter cleanse.

Drain and thoroughly rinse the chickpeas. Set aside.

Heat the olive oil in a large saucepan over medium heat, add the onion,
celery and carrot and a generous pinch of salt and sauté, stirring
occasionally, for 10 minutes to soften the vegetables. Stir in the garlic, bay
leaves, thyme and a pinch of black pepper and cook for another 30 seconds.

Add the chickpeas to the pan, pour in 2 litres of water and bring to the boil.
Reduce the heat to low, cover and simmer, skimming off any white froth
that rises to the surface, for 1½ hours or until the chickpeas are tender.
Remove from the heat.

Transfer 750 ml (3 cups) of soup to a food processor, add the lemon juice
and blitz to form a puree (if you prefer a thicker consistency you can puree
more soup).

Stir the puree back into the soup to thicken it. Taste and adjust the
seasoning as required. Spoon the soup into bowls, scatter on the chopped
herbs, add a drizzle of olive oil and serve.

NOTE
—Salting chickpeas at the beginning of the cooking process is
controversial. Some people believe it toughens them, but I find
if you don't add the salt early, the chickpeas and vegetables taste
bland and are not seasoned from within.

Fasolada
White Bean Soup

250 g dried cannellini beans, soaked overnight in water

80 ml (⅓ cup) extra-virgin olive oil, plus extra for drizzling

1 onion, finely chopped

1 large carrot, cut into 5 mm thick rounds

1 celery stalk, cut into 1 cm thick slices

sea salt flakes and freshly ground black pepper

2 garlic cloves, finely chopped

1 tablespoon tomato paste

200 g canned crushed tomatoes

2 fresh bay leaves

1 whole red apple

pinch of chilli flakes (optional)

DF, GF, VG | **SERVES 4–6**

Rustic tomato and bean soups are prevalent throughout the Mediterranean. They even have similar names – fasoulia in Arabic, fagiolata in Italian and fabada in Spanish. In ancient times peasants relied on these cheap, but certainly never lacking in flavour, protein- and fibre-rich plant-based soups to nourish them. In this hearty soup, creamy white beans, tender carrot and sweet celery swim in a delicious tomato broth – you can even spice things up with a pinch of chilli flakes. For some added body and a touch of sweetness, add a whole red apple when the soup is simmering. The apple's pectin works as a thickening agent, resulting in a lovely velvety texture.

Drain and thoroughly rinse the beans, then place them in a large saucepan and cover with plenty of cold water. Bring to the boil, then reduce the heat to low, cover and simmer for 30 minutes. Drain and set aside.

Clean the pan, then place over low heat. Add the olive oil, onion, carrot, celery and a generous pinch of salt and sauté, stirring occasionally, for 15 minutes to soften the vegetables. Add the garlic and tomato paste and cook for another 30 seconds.

Add the beans, crushed tomatoes, bay leaves, apple, chilli flakes (if using), a pinch of salt and pepper and 1 litre of hot water to the pan. Cover and simmer for 1 hour. Remove the apple, taste and adjust the seasoning as required. Serve the soup in bowls, with an extra drizzle of olive oil and a sprinkle of pepper.

Mejadra
Lentils with Rice & Crispy Onion

200 g brown lentils, rinsed

3 tablespoons extra-virgin olive oil

3 onions, finely sliced

sea salt flakes and freshly ground black pepper

2 teaspoons cumin seeds

2 teaspoons coriander seeds

1 teaspoon ground cinnamon

150 g (¾ cup) basmati rice, rinsed

875 ml (3½ cups) boiling water

CRISPY ONION

1 large onion, finely sliced into rings

light olive oil, for shallow-frying

DF, GF, VG | SERVES 6–8

My Lebanese friends introduced me to mejadra when I was in high school. I instantly fell in love with the simple combination of caramelised onion, rice and lentils topped with crispy onion. Each Lebanese family in the neighbourhood had their own treasured version of this recipe: some added aromatic spices, while others simply seasoned theirs with salt. Personally, I love the fragrant combination of warming cumin, coriander and cinnamon with the rice and lentils. Delicious as a stand-alone vegan meal or a side dish as part of a buffet.

Place the lentils in a saucepan and cover with plenty of water. Bring to the boil, reduce the heat to low and simmer for 12 minutes to soften. Drain and set aside.

Meanwhile, heat a large frying pan over medium–low heat. Add the olive oil and onion and a generous pinch of salt and cook, stirring regularly, for 15 minutes or until the onion is caramelised. Stir in the cumin and coriander seeds and cinnamon and cook for a further 1 minute to toast the spices.

Add the rice, lentils and a pinch of salt and pepper to the pan, stir to combine, and cook for 1 minute. Pour in the boiling water, reduce the heat to low, cover and simmer for 10 minutes. Check the mixture and add a little more water if the pan looks dry, then cook for a further 5 minutes until all the liquid has been absorbed. Turn off the heat. Lift the lid, cover the pan with a tea towel, then replace the lid. (The towel absorbs the moisture to keep the mixture light and fluffy.) Rest for 10 minutes.

To make the crispy onion, dry the onion rings with paper towel to remove excess moisture. Heat enough light olive oil for shallow-frying in a frying pan over medium–high heat, add the onion rings and cook for 5 minutes or until golden and crispy. Drain on paper towel and sprinkle with salt while hot.

To serve, transfer the mejadra to a platter and top with the crispy onion.

Ta'ameya
Egyptian Falafel

300 g dried fava beans (also known as dried broad beans)

½ teaspoon bicarbonate of soda

5 spring onions, sliced

4 garlic cloves, finely chopped

large handful of flat-leaf parsley leaves, finely chopped

large handful of coriander leaves, finely chopped

2 teaspoons sea salt flakes

1 teaspoon ground cumin

1 teaspoon ground coriander

¼ teaspoon cayenne pepper (optional)

1 teaspoon gluten-free baking powder

2 tablespoons sesame seeds

sunflower oil, for deep-frying

Tahini Sauce (page 211) or Hummus (page 210), to serve

DF, GF, VG | MAKES 20

Throughout the Mediterranean, falafel recipes vary from country to country. Egyptians make their falafels with only fava beans, while other Middle Eastern countries use chickpeas or a combination of both. While chickpeas have a wonderful nutty flavour, they are much drier than fava beans, so the fritters are not as moist and fluffy. Loaded with aromatic spices and fresh herbs for vivid colour, these vegan ta'ameya are incredibly easy to make and are far superior to store-bought varieties. My ultimate falafel is ultra crispy on the outside and vibrant green and fluffy on the inside.

For a nourishing vegan meal, serve – plated or wrapped in soft gluten-free Pita Bread (page 24) – with tabbouleh (page 47) and your favourite sauce.

Place the fava beans and bicarbonate of soda in a large bowl and add plenty of water. Set aside to soak overnight. The next day, drain and rinse the fava beans thoroughly.

Transfer the fava beans to a food processor and blitz to make a coarse meal. Add the spring onion, garlic, herbs, salt, spices and baking powder and blitz, stopping occasionally to scrape down the side of the bowl, until you have a coarse paste. Transfer to a bowl, fold in the sesame seeds, cover and rest in the fridge for 30 minutes.

Using either your hands or a falafel scooper, shape the fava bean mixture into 20 golf ball–sized patties.

Heat enough sunflower oil for deep-frying in a large, deep frying pan until it reaches 180°C on a kitchen thermometer (or until a cube of gluten-free bread dropped in the oil browns in 15 seconds). Working in three batches, fry the falafel for 4 minutes or until golden and crispy. Remove with a slotted spoon and drain on paper towel. Cool slightly and serve with tahini sauce or hummus.

NOTE
—Uncooked falafel can be kept in an airtight container and frozen for up to 6 months. You might like to fry half this batch and freeze half for later use.

Arakas Laderos
Tomato-braised Peas & Vegetables

125 ml (½ cup) extra-virgin olive oil

1 onion, finely chopped

sea salt flakes and freshly ground black pepper

2 garlic cloves, finely chopped

1 tablespoon tomato paste

2 carrots, cut into 1 cm rounds

2 waxy potatoes (such as desiree or pontiac), cut into 4 cm cubes

400 g can crushed tomatoes

500 g frozen peas

handful of dill fronds, finely chopped

crusty gluten-free rolls, to serve

Greek feta, to serve (optional)

DFO, GF, V, VGO | SERVES 4–6

This is one of those classic wintery dishes that is delicious as a stand-alone vegan meal or as an accompaniment to roast meat. 'Laderos' refers to good-quality extra-virgin olive oil, which forms the basis of the stew, and 'arakas' refers to peas, the star of the dish. You can prepare this meal with peas alone or a medley of vegetables, just be careful not to add too much liquid when simmering your vegetables, otherwise your tomato broth will be watery, rather than rich and oily. The addition of fresh dill to finish gives the dish grassy citrus notes. It's delicious when paired with a chunk of creamy, salted feta and crusty gluten-free bread rolls for mopping up the sauce.

Heat the olive oil in a saucepan over medium–low heat. Add the onion and a pinch of salt and sauté, stirring occasionally, for 8 minutes to soften. Add the garlic and tomato paste and cook for another 30 seconds.

Add the carrot, potato, crushed tomatoes and 500 ml (2 cups) of water to the pan and season with a pinch of salt and pepper. Bring to the boil, reduce the heat to low, cover and simmer for 20 minutes. Add the peas and simmer for another 10 minutes or until the potato is tender.

Take the pan off the heat and stir through the dill. Taste and adjust the seasoning as required. Serve with crusty gluten-free rolls and feta (if using) on the side.

Piperies Me Feta
Roasted Bullhorn Capsicums Stuffed with Feta

300 g Greek feta

generous pinch of dried oregano

sea salt flakes and freshly ground black pepper

6 red and yellow bullhorn capsicums

2 tablespoons extra-virgin olive oil

balsamic vinegar, for drizzling

finely chopped flat-leaf parsley leaves, to serve

DFO, GF, V | **SERVES 6**

Oozy, creamy melted feta encased in sweet, caramelised capsicums and drizzled with balsamic vinegar for a little acidic kick – what an extraordinary combination. Roasted capsicums are fantastic for a dinner party because they are ridiculously easy to prepare, deliver big flavour and are visually stunning. Yellow capsicums taste milder and sweeter than red; I like to use a combination of both, but you can use whichever you prefer.

Preheat the oven to 200°C (fan-forced). Line a baking tray with baking paper.

Combine the feta, oregano and a pinch of black pepper in a bowl.

Half slice across the top of each capsicum to create an opening. Using your knife, remove the seeds and membranes inside the capsicums and rinse to clean the interior. Use a small spoon to stuff the capsicums with the feta mixture, ensuring you push the cheese all the way down to the bottom (allow a small gap at the top to prevent the melted cheese from oozing out). Close the lids and pierce with toothpicks to secure them in place.

Place the capsicums on the prepared tray. Drizzle the olive oil over the capsicums, sprinkle on a pinch of salt and roast for 25–30 minutes or until blistered. Serve the capsicums on the tray or transfer to a platter. Drizzle balsamic vinegar over the top, then scatter with parsley to serve.

VARIATION

— For a dairy-free version, omit the feta stuffing – the roasted capsicums are still delicious on their own drizzled with balsamic vinegar and scattered with parsley.

Vegan Moussaka

2 eggplants, finely sliced, patted dry

2 zucchini, finely sliced, patted dry

extra-virgin olive oil, for pan-frying

2 large all-purpose potatoes (such as sebago), peeled, finely sliced and steamed (see Note)

TOMATO SAUCE

3 tablespoons extra-virgin olive oil

1 onion, finely diced

sea salt flakes and freshly ground black pepper

3 garlic cloves, finely chopped

2 tablespoons tomato paste

80 ml (⅓ cup) red wine

400 g can crushed tomatoes

1 teaspoon dried oregano

PUMPKIN & CAULIFLOWER MASH

600 g butternut pumpkin, peeled and cut into 3 cm cubes

400 g cauliflower, broken into florets

2 tablespoons extra-virgin olive oil

pinch of ground cinnamon

1 teaspoon sea salt flakes

DF, GF, VG | SERVES 8

During religious fasting periods many iconic Greek dishes are given a vegan makeover to eliminate animal products. This is my healthy and delicious vegan moussaka. You get all those familiar flavours, but instead of a creamy bechamel, I finish it with a light and fluffy vegetable mash – and it works beautifully. Loaded with vegetables, this express moussaka is a good option any time of the year when you want something hearty and comforting. You can assemble the moussaka a day ahead if you wish and just pop it in the oven after work.

To make the tomato sauce, heat the olive oil in a large saucepan over medium heat. Add the onion and a pinch of salt and sauté, stirring occasionally, for 10 minutes or until softened. Add the garlic and tomato paste and cook for another minute. Deglaze the pan with the red wine, stirring to release any caramelised bits caught on the base, and simmer for 1 minute or until reduced by half. Stir in the crushed tomatoes, oregano and 125 ml (½ cup) of water and season with black pepper. Reduce the heat to low, cover and simmer for 20 minutes. Taste and adjust the seasoning, if necessary.

While the sauce is simmering, sprinkle the eggplant and zucchini slices with salt and set aside to rest for 5 minutes (this reduces the bitterness). Pat dry. Place a frying pan over medium–high heat, drizzle in some olive oil and pan-fry the eggplant and zucchini separately and in batches until golden on both sides, adding more oil as needed. Drain on paper towel.

To make the mash, cook the pumpkin in a large saucepan of salted boiling water for 5 minutes. Add the cauliflower and simmer for another 10 minutes. Drain well, then transfer the vegetables to a food processor. Add the olive oil, cinnamon and salt and blitz to form a smooth mash.

Preheat the oven to 200°C (fan-forced). Grease a 30 cm × 25 cm deep roasting dish.

To assemble the moussaka, spread a ladleful of tomato sauce over the base of the dish. Arrange the eggplant slices on top of the tomato sauce, then follow with the zucchini slices. Top with the remaining tomato sauce. Arrange the potato slices on top of the sauce and cover with the mash. Bake for 35 minutes or until golden. Remove from the oven and let the moussaka rest for 10 minutes before slicing and serving.

NOTE
—The potato slices can be steamed in the microwave or in a steamer basket on the stovetop. Steam for about 10 minutes to par cook.

Briam
Roasted Vegetables

2 large all-purpose potatoes (such as sebago), cut into 4 cm chunks

1 large eggplant or 2 zucchini, cut into 4 cm chunks

2 small capsicums (1 red, 1 yellow), cut into 4 cm chunks

2 large tomatoes, grated, skins discarded

1 red onion, quartered and layers separated

2 garlic cloves, finely chopped

2 teaspoons dried oregano

sea salt flakes and freshly ground black pepper

80 ml (⅓ cup) extra-virgin olive oil

finely chopped flat-leaf parsley leaves, to serve

DF, GF, VG | SERVES 4–6

The French call it ratatouille; the Greeks call it tourlou tourlou, but have also adopted the more commonly used Turkish name, briam. Regardless, this is essentially the same vegan dish – a rainbow of nutrient-dense vegetables roasted in olive oil and tomato with slight variations from country to country. You can add any leftover veggies in your fridge; carrots and cauliflower work well. Briam is a must at any Mediterranean buffet, so feel free to double or triple the recipe to feed a crowd.

Preheat the oven to 180°C (fan-forced).

Place all the vegetables and garlic in a roasting tin and season with the oregano and a generous sprinkling of salt and black pepper. Pour on the olive oil and 125 ml (½ cup) of water and toss to combine.

Bake the briam for 1 hour or until golden, tossing halfway through for even cooking. Scatter parsley on top and serve.

NOTES

— I prefer to use the flesh of grated tomato for a fresher, lighter flavour in this recipe. If you don't have fresh tomatoes, you can use 200 g canned crushed tomatoes instead.

— It is important to cut your veggies into equal-sized pieces so they cook at the same speed.

Horta
Wild Leafy Greens

1 kg wild greens (such as chicory, endive or amaranth)

3 tablespoons extra-virgin olive oil

juice of 1 small lemon

pinch of sea salt flakes

DF, GF, VG | **SERVES 4–6**

I wasn't game enough to try horta until I was 18. The thought of eating wild green leaves my mother had picked from our backyard didn't exactly appeal to me as a kid, but once I sampled their pure, clean taste I was converted. Horta are so simple to prepare: just simmer until wilted, then bathe in the best-quality extra-virgin olive oil and the juice of a lemon and you have a healthy and delicious accompaniment to fish or any grilled protein. The leaves will significantly reduce in size while cooking, so don't be alarmed by the large volume going into the saucepan. I love horta served warm with a chunk of feta or silky skordalia on the side, but they can also be served at room temperature.

Thoroughly wash the greens. Cut the long stalks in half and trim off any very coarse stems.

Place the greens in a large saucepan of well salted boiling water. Simmer for 10–15 minutes or until the stalks are tender, but not overcooked. Drain well and transfer the greens to a platter. Immediately dress the hot greens with the olive oil, lemon juice and salt so they can soak up the dressing. Serve warm or at room temperature.

NUTRITION NOTE
—Wild greens are an ancient low-calorie 'superfood'. They are rich in antioxidants and phytonutrients, fibre, vitamin K, iron, calcium and other minerals.

Papoutsakia
Stuffed Eggplant

3 eggplants, cut in half lengthways, flesh scored deeply in a crisscross pattern

sea salt flakes and freshly ground black pepper

80 ml (⅓ cup) extra-virgin olive oil

1 onion, finely chopped

3 garlic cloves, finely chopped

2 tablespoons tomato paste

250 g beef mince

1 teaspoon dried oregano

1 teaspoon ground cinnamon

½ teaspoon ground cloves

½ teaspoon caster sugar

3 tablespoons red wine

400 g can crushed tomatoes

handful of flat-leaf parsley leaves, finely chopped, plus extra to serve

40 g pecorino or parmigiano reggiano, finely grated

BECHAMEL

20 g butter

1 tablespoon gluten-free plain flour

330 ml (1⅓ cups) milk

200 g kefalotyri or kefalograviera cheese, grated

pinch of grated nutmeg

GF, VO | **SERVES 4–6**

'Papoutsakia' means 'little shoes' in Greek. When I was a kid, I thought it was hilarious that I was eating a shoe! Papoutsakia taste similar to a deconstructed moussaka – with all those familiar flavours of roasted eggplant, rich bolognese and cheesy bechamel – but they can be prepared in a fraction of the time.

Preheat the oven to 200°C (fan-forced).

Place the eggplant in a large roasting tin, season with salt and pepper and drizzle on half the olive oil. Massage the seasoning all over the eggplant and arrange, scored-side down, in the tin. Roast for 30 minutes to soften.

While the eggplant is roasting, prepare your filling. Heat the remaining oil in a frying pan over medium–low heat. Add the onion and a pinch of salt and sauté, stirring occasionally, for 5 minutes to soften. Stir in the garlic and tomato paste and cook for another minute.

Add the mince to the pan and allow it to sear for a minute to form a crust before breaking it up with a wooden spoon. Add the oregano, cinnamon, cloves, sugar and a pinch of salt and pepper. Cook for 1 minute to caramelise the meat and toast the spices, then stir in the red wine and simmer for a few minutes until reduced by half. Add the tomatoes and 125 ml (½ cup) of water, then cover and simmer for 15 minutes to thicken the sauce. Remove the pan from the heat.

Remove the eggplant from the oven and turn the pieces over so the flesh side is facing up. Using a spoon, carefully scoop out the flesh and add it to the mince sauce along with the parsley. Stir to combine, taste and adjust the seasoning as required. Spoon the mince filling into the eggplant cavities.

To make the bechamel, melt the butter in a small saucepan over medium–low heat. Add the flour and whisk until a paste forms. Slowly pour in the milk, whisking continuously for a few minutes until the sauce is thick and creamy. Add the cheese and nutmeg, stir well until the cheese has melted and remove from the heat.

Spoon the bechamel over each stuffed eggplant half and finish with a sprinkling of pecorino or parmigiano. Return the eggplant to the oven and cook for a further 20 minutes or until the papoutsakia are golden. Scatter with parsley and serve.

VARIATION
—For an equally delicious vegetarian version, simply replace the beef with roughly chopped mushrooms.

RICE

POTA

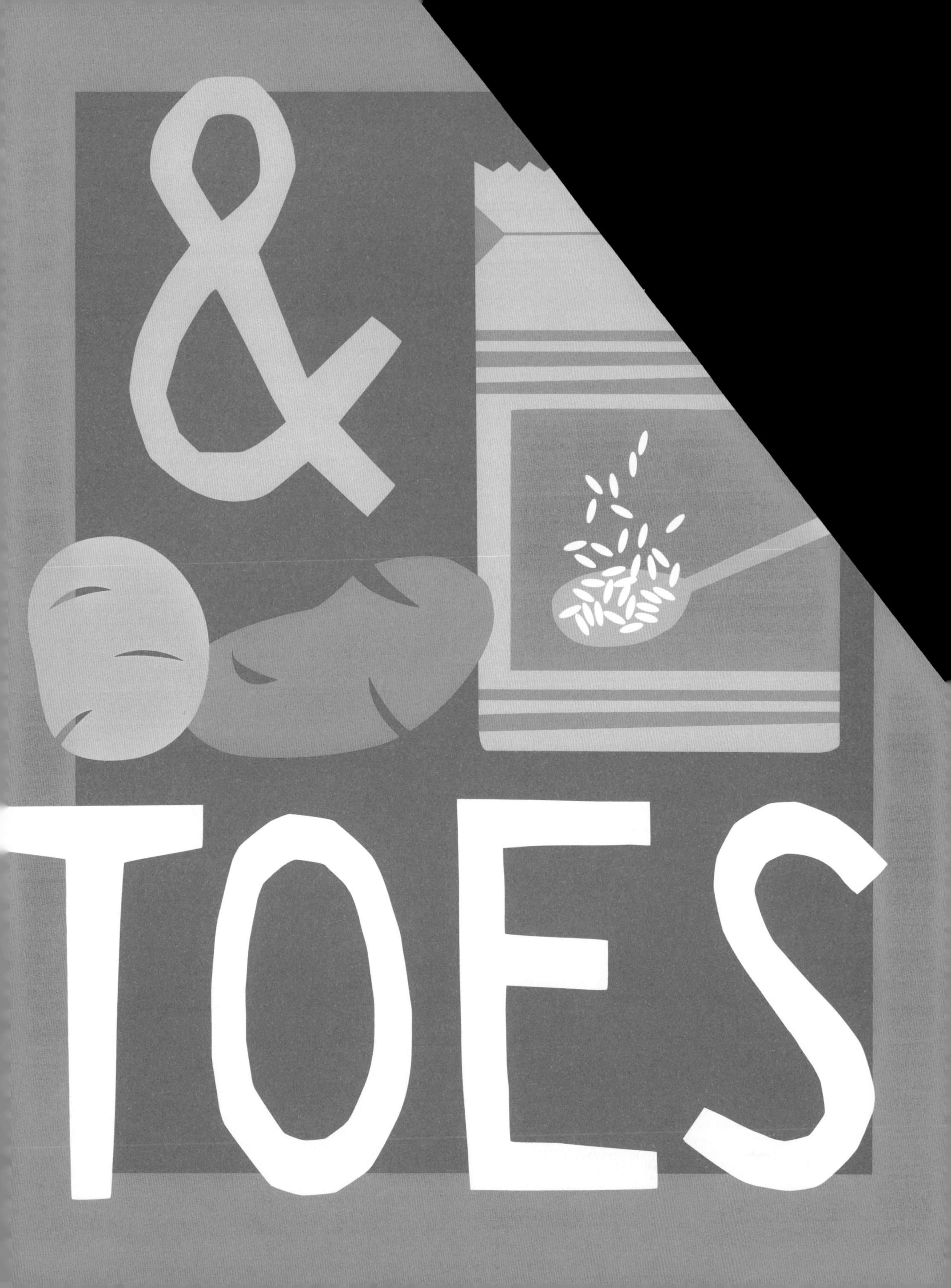
&
TOES

...ella

... for a lengthy list of ingredients that
..., a major turn-off for most home
... complicated. My version is very
... cious. Rice is the star of the show,
... stock of smoky paprika, floral saffron
... and mussels are then nestled into
... f succulent seafood and further
... of a great paella is the 'socarrat',
... m of the pan that everyone fights
... eat in the last few minutes of
... crunch.

... low heat. Add the olive oil,
... sauté, stirring occasionally, for
... the garlic and paprika and cook for another

... tract

... mussels, cleaned and
debearded

50 g (⅓ cup) frozen peas

handful of flat leaf parsley leaves,
finely chopped

lemon wedges, to serve

DF, GF | **SERVES 4**

Add the rice to the pan and stir for a few seconds to coat the grains in the
oil. Stir in the stock, tomato and saffron and season with a pinch of salt and
pepper. Bring to a simmer and cook gently for 10 minutes without stirring.

Nestle the prawns and mussels in the rice and scatter on the peas. Cover
and simmer for 5 minutes or until most of the stock is absorbed and the
rice is al dente. Remove the lid and increase the heat to high. Cook for
2 minutes to achieve the 'socarrat' crust on the base, then remove the pan
from the heat, cover and rest for 5 minutes. Scatter on the parsley and serve
with lemon wedges.

Lahanorizo
Cabbage, Leek & Rice Stew

80 ml (⅓ cup) extra-virgin olive oil, plus extra for drizzling

1 small onion, finely chopped

1 small leek, white and green parts, finely sliced

sea salt flakes and freshly ground black pepper

1 tablespoon tomato paste

1 garlic clove, finely chopped

400 g white cabbage, finely shredded

110 g (½ cup) short-grain rice

1 vine-ripened tomato

squeeze of lemon juice

large handful of dill fronds, finely chopped

DF, GF, VG | **SERVES 4**

Lahanorizo is a delicious one-pot vegan stew of shredded cabbage (lahano), leeks and rice (rizi). Braising the cabbage and leek enhances their natural sweetness, transforming them from crispy vegetables into something meltingly tender in under 20 minutes. I make this stew in the cooler months as a stand-alone meal, but you can also prepare it as a warming side dish to complement grilled proteins.

Heat the olive oil in a large saucepan over medium–low heat. Add the onion, leek and a generous pinch of salt and sauté, stirring occasionally, for 5 minutes to soften. Stir in the tomato paste and garlic and cook for another 30 seconds.

Add the cabbage to the pan and sauté, stirring occasionally to ensure the cabbage doesn't burn, for 8 minutes to soften. Add the rice, along with a pinch of black pepper, and grate in the flesh and juice of the tomato, discarding the skin. Reduce the heat to low, pour in 1 litre of water, then cover and simmer for 15 minutes until the rice is cooked through and the water is absorbed. Remove from the heat and stir in the lemon juice and dill. Taste and adjust the seasoning as required. Spoon the lahanorizo into bowls and serve with a drizzle of extra olive oil.

VARIATION

— If dairy isn't an issue, serve with Greek feta crumbled over the top and watch the cheese ooze into the rice – simply delicious.

Oozy Vegan Pumpkin & Saffron Risotto

400 g butternut pumpkin, peeled and cut into 1.5 cm cubes

80 ml (⅓ cup) extra-virgin olive oil

sea salt flakes and freshly ground black pepper

875 ml (3½ cups) warm Vegetable Stock (page 207)

1 onion, finely chopped

2 garlic cloves, finely chopped

275 g (1¼ cups) arborio or carnaroli rice

pinch of saffron threads

125 ml (½ cup) white wine

crispy sage leaves, to serve (optional) (see Note)

DF, GF, VG | SERVES 4

Oozy is not a word you would normally associate with a risotto made without butter or cheese. The secret here is caramelised roasted pumpkin that is pureed to add a smooth, creamy texture and delicate sweetness to the risotto. Earthy, floral saffron complements the pumpkin's sweetness and produces a sunny, golden risotto. Ensure you use a short-grain high-starch rice, such as arborio or carnaroli, for that signature creamy texture.

Preheat the oven to 180°C (fan-forced).

Place 250 g of the pumpkin in a roasting tin, drizzle in half the olive oil, add a pinch of salt and toss well. Roast for 30 minutes, tossing halfway through to ensure even browning. Transfer the pumpkin to a food processor, add 80 ml (⅓ cup) of the stock and puree. Set aside.

Meanwhile, heat the remaining oil in a large frying pan over medium–low heat. Add the onion and a generous pinch of salt and cook for 5 minutes to soften. Stir in the garlic and cook for another 30 seconds. Add the remaining pumpkin, the rice and saffron and gently stir for a minute to toast the rice grains.

Deglaze the pan with the white wine, stirring to release any caramelised bits caught on the base, and simmer for a minute so the rice absorbs the wine. Add a few ladles of the remaining stock and bring to a gentle simmer. When the stock has been absorbed, add more to the pan, a few ladles at a time. Continue, gradually adding more stock as it is absorbed, and cook for 15 minutes or until the rice is al dente. In the last 2 minutes of simmering, gently fold in the pumpkin puree. Remove the pan from the heat and adjust the seasoning with salt and pepper as required. Ladle the risotto into shallow bowls and serve with crispy sage leaves scattered over the top, if desired.

NOTE

—Crispy sage leaves: fry a handful of sage leaves in 3 tablespoons of olive oil over medium heat for 30 seconds or until crisp. Remove with a slotted spoon and sprinkle with salt.

Cretan Wedding Pilaf

1 x 1.5 kg chicken

sea salt flakes and freshly ground black pepper

400 g (2 cups) medium-grain rice

juice of 1 lemon

30 g butter (optional)

DFO, GF | SERVES 6

When I was a young adult I was fortunate enough to attend a Cretan wedding in my mother's hometown of Hania. It was a very loud and memorable night of dancing and feasting with 600 other guests. The food memory that stood out was the large platters of prized Cretan wedding pilaf, a traditional dish served to guests that symbolises fertility and good luck for the newlyweds. The texture was wet and oozy like a risotto, the creaminess derived from the gelatinous meat stock in which the rice had simmered. Wedding pilaf can be prepared with goat, lamb or chicken. My mother makes the chicken version most often at home because it is the easiest and universally loved. Her recipe requires only a handful of ingredients but produces one of the creamiest and most flavoursome rice dishes you will ever make. Like risotto, for the ooziest texture, pilaf needs to be eaten as soon as it is made.

Place the chicken in a stockpot or large saucepan and add 2 litres of water. Add a very generous pinch of salt and bring to the boil. Reduce the heat to low, cover and simmer for 1–1½ hours or until the chicken is tender and the stock is gelatinous.

Remove the chicken from the pan and strain 1.5 litres of the stock into another saucepan. Store any remaining stock in an airtight container in the fridge for up to 4 days or freeze for up to 6 months.

Add the rice to the stock, place over low heat and simmer, stirring occasionally, for 13 minutes or until the rice is al dente (it will continue to cook while it rests so don't overcook it). Pour in the lemon juice, taste and adjust the seasoning with salt and black pepper, as required. At this point you can add the butter for extra creaminess. Cover the pan and let the pilaf rest for 5 minutes before transferring it to a platter. Remove the flesh from the chicken and serve alongside the pilaf. Finish with a grinding of black pepper to serve.

Vegetarian Dolmades
Stuffed Vine Leaves

25 fresh vine leaves

125 ml (½ cup) extra-virgin olive oil

1 small red onion, grated and moisture squeezed out

2 spring onions, finely sliced

1 tablespoon sea salt flakes

¼ teaspoon ground cumin

1 large vine-ripened tomato, grated, skin discarded

pinch of freshly ground black pepper

200 g (1 cup) medium-grain rice, rinsed

handful of mint leaves, finely chopped

handful of flat-leaf parsley leaves, finely chopped

2 tablespoons dill fronds, finely chopped

2 tablespoons pine nuts, toasted

lemon wedges and Tzatziki (page 208) or Greek yoghurt (or coconut yoghurt), to serve

DFO, GF, V, VGO | SERVES 4–8

As much as I love meat-filled dolmades, in summer I prefer a lighter vegetarian version of these delicious bites of heaven. The vibrant trio of fresh mint, dill and parsley, combined with freshly grated tomato to brighten the filling, is all you need for moist, flavour-crammed dolmades. A sprinkling of toasted pine nuts adds beautiful textural crunch, but feel free to omit for a nut-free version. I use fresh vine leaves from my mother's garden for the best taste and texture – you can usually buy fresh leaves at your local Mediterranean grocer in the summer months. If you are using the packaged variety out of season, there's no need to blanch them – just rinse them thoroughly and drain prior to use.

Working in batches, blanch the vine leaves in a saucepan of salted boiling water for 30 seconds. Remove with tongs and drain in a large colander.

Heat 3 tablespoons of the olive oil in a large frying pan over low heat, add the onion, spring onion, salt and cumin and cook, stirring occasionally, for 5 minutes or until softened. Stir in the tomato and black pepper and cook for 3 minutes. Add the rice, chopped herbs and pine nuts and cook for another minute.

Sort through the vine leaves and set aside any that are torn. Place the remaining leaves on a chopping board, vein-side up. Place 1 tablespoon of the filling at the base of each leaf, then roll up, folding in the sides, to form logs about 5 cm long.

Cover the bottom of a large wide saucepan with the reserved torn leaves to prevent the dolmades from burning and sticking to the base. Place the dolmades in the pan, seam-side down, sitting next to each other. Continue with a second layer. Drizzle the remaining oil over the dolmades and pour 560 ml (2¼ cups) of water down the side of the pan. Place a dinner plate face down on the dolmades so they don't open during cooking.

Cover with a lid and gently simmer over low heat for 40 minutes or until all the water has been absorbed. Remove from the heat and rest for 10 minutes. Serve the dolmades with lemon wedges and a dollop of tzatziki or yoghurt.

NOTE

— Double this recipe if making for a celebration or large event.

Yemista
Stuffed Vegetables

6 large tomatoes

4 small capsicums (various colours)

sea salt flakes and freshly ground black pepper

125 ml (½ cup) extra-virgin olive oil

1 small onion, diced

2 garlic cloves, finely chopped

200 g beef mince

100 g (½ cup) medium-grain rice

1 teaspoon dried oregano, plus extra for sprinkling

¼ teaspoon ground cinnamon

¼ teaspoon ground allspice

handful of flat-leaf parsley leaves, finely chopped

handful of dill fronds, finely chopped

handful of mint leaves, finely chopped

2 large all-purpose potatoes (such as sebago), peeled and cut into wedges

DF, GF, VGO | SERVES 6–8

Yemista are vegetables stuffed with rice, mince and vibrant green herbs ('yemisi' translates to 'fill or stuff' in Greek). Personally, tomatoes are my favourite vegetables to stuff (and the most popular) because the acidity of the tender baked tomatoes perfectly balances the starchy filling. Other popular vegetables to fill include capsicum, zucchini and eggplant – onions also work. I love to add fragrant spices like cinnamon and allspice to my filling for a more complex flavour.

Preheat the oven to 180°C (fan-forced).

Slice off the top quarter of each tomato and capsicum to create a lid. Set aside the lids and scoop out the tomato flesh with a spoon (be careful not to break the shell). Blitz the flesh in a food processor to make a tomato puree and set aside. Remove the core of each capsicum and clean the inside of the shell. Place the vegetable shells upright in a roasting tin and sprinkle a pinch of salt and pepper inside each shell.

To make the filling, heat 2 tablespoons of the olive oil in a large frying pan over medium–low heat. Add the onion and a pinch of salt and sauté, stirring occasionally, for 5 minutes to soften. Add the garlic and cook for a further 30 seconds. Add the mince to the pan and brown for 2–3 minutes, breaking it up with a wooden spoon. Stir in the rice and cook, stirring occasionally, for a minute so it toasts (this prevents it from turning soggy). Add the reserved tomato puree, oregano, cinnamon, allspice and a generous pinch of salt and pepper. Let the mixture simmer and reduce for 5 minutes. Remove the pan from the heat and stir through the herbs. Taste and adjust the seasoning as required.

Spoon the filling into the vegetable shells until roughly three-quarters full (allow some room for the rice to expand). Place the lids on the vegetables and sit the potato wedges between the vegetables to help them stay upright. Sprinkle salt and a pinch of extra oregano over the potato. Drizzle the remaining oil over the vegetables and pour 250 ml (1 cup) of water down the side of the tin to help cook the potatoes. Tightly seal the tin with foil and bake for 45 minutes. Uncover and bake for another 45 minutes or until the vegetables are golden and the rice is tender.

VARIATION

— For equally delicious vegan yemista, simply omit the mince and replace with an extra 50 g (¼ cup) of rice.

Patatas Bravas
Crispy Roasted Potatoes

1.2 kg all-purpose potatoes (such as sebago), peeled and cut into large chunks

sea salt flakes

3 tablespoons extra-virgin olive oil

SPICY TOMATO SAUCE

3 tablespoons extra-virgin olive oil

1 small onion, roughly chopped

1 long red chilli, deseeded and finely sliced (add more for extra heat)

sea salt flakes

1 garlic clove, roughly chopped

1 teaspoon smoked paprika

½ teaspoon caster sugar

2 large tomatoes, chopped

1 teaspoon sherry vinegar

finely chopped chives, to serve

DF, GF, VG | **SERVES 4–6**

Patatas bravas are an iconic Spanish tapa, usually potatoes fried in olive oil until golden and crispy. My husband loves patatas bravas and at home – as a healthier alternative, and without compromising on serious crunch – I prefer to bake them. These delicious potatoes are so crispy they actually taste fried. The key to achieving incredible crunch is to parboil your potatoes first, so they go light and fluffy on the inside. Next, drain them and rough them up with a good shake so the edges can crisp up when they are finished off in a hot oven. While the potatoes are baking, you can quickly whiz up your spicy tomato sauce ready for drizzling. Done!

To parboil the potato chunks, place them in a saucepan, cover with cold water and add a generous pinch of salt. Bring to the boil, reduce the heat to medium–low and simmer for 15 minutes or until softened on the edges. Drain the potato chunks in a colander, then vigorously shake to rough up the edges (fluffy broken edges equal crispy potatoes). Let them rest for 15 minutes so the steam escapes.

Preheat the oven to 220°C (fan-forced).

Transfer the potato to a roasting tin in a single layer. Add the olive oil and a pinch of salt and toss to combine. Bake for 45–50 minutes or until the potato is golden and crispy, tossing halfway through.

Meanwhile, to make the spicy tomato sauce, heat the olive oil in a small frying pan over low heat. Add the onion, chilli and a pinch of salt and cook for 5 minutes to soften. Add the remaining sauce ingredients and simmer for another 5 minutes. Remove the pan from the heat, then transfer the sauce to a food processor and blitz to a puree.

Place the crispy potato chunks on a platter, drizzle with the sauce and sprinkle with chives. Serve immediately.

Patates Lemonates
Waxy Lemon Oregano Potatoes

1.2 kg waxy potatoes (such as desiree or pontiac), cut into wedges

1½ teaspoons dried oregano

1 tablespoon sea salt flakes

pinch of freshly ground white pepper

375 ml (1½ cups) Chicken Stock (page 206) or water

80 ml (⅓ cup) extra-virgin olive oil

juice of 1 small lemon

DF, GF, VGO | **SERVES 4–6**

Incredibly simple but tasty, these potatoes are the must-have side dish at every barbecue. First, ensure you purchase the correct type of potato – you want the waxy texture of a desiree or pontiac – that softens nicely but still holds its shape. Second, ensure there is enough liquid in the tin, so the snug potato wedges braise nicely – they need to be almost submerged. Perfect these two simple rules and your potatoes will be wonderfully flavourful every time.

Preheat the oven to 180°C (fan-forced).

Place the potato wedges snugly in a 30 cm × 25 cm roasting tin. Sprinkle with the oregano, salt and white pepper. Add the stock or water, olive oil and lemon juice and toss to combine (the potato wedges should be almost submerged in the liquid; if not, add some water).

Braise the potato wedges, tossing them a few times to ensure even browning, for 1½ hours or until soft and golden. Taste and adjust the seasoning as required, then serve immediately.

NOTE

— If you don't have any chicken stock, add a gluten-free chicken stock cube to the liquid in the tin for a flavour boost.

PASTA

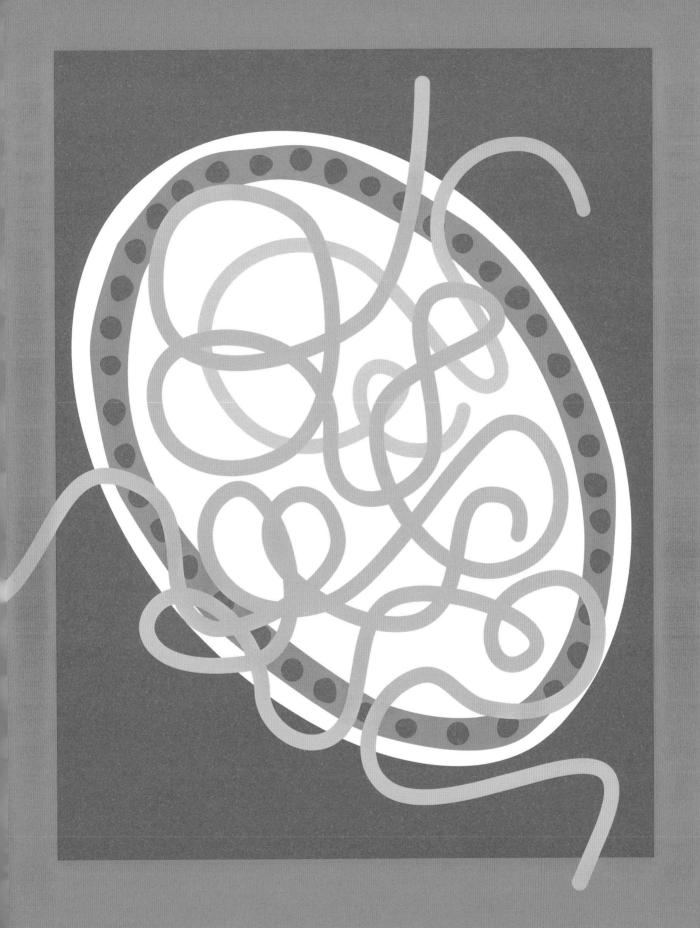

Corfu's Pastitsada
Chicken in Rich Tomato Sauce

4 chicken marylands

sea salt flakes and freshly ground black pepper

2 tablespoons extra-virgin olive oil

1 large onion, finely chopped

5 garlic cloves, finely sliced

2 tablespoons tomato paste

3 fresh bay leaves

1 tablespoon thyme leaves

1 teaspoon dried oregano

2 cinnamon sticks

6 allspice berries

3 whole cloves

250 ml (1 cup) red wine

400 g can crushed tomatoes

320 g gluten-free casarecce (or other chunky pasta)

handful of flat-leaf parsley leaves, finely chopped

grated myzithra cheese or parmigiano reggiano, to serve (optional)

DFO, GF | **SERVES 4**

Corfu, one of the lush green Ionian islands, sits west of mainland Greece. Historically, the island was ruled by the Venetians, so it retains a strong Italian influence in both food and architecture. Pastitsada, one of Corfu's most iconic dishes, is derived from the Venetian dish pastizzada – a tomato-based stew made with chicken or beef and scented with a warming aromatic mix of allspice, cinnamon, bay leaf and clove. Traditionally served with thick strands of bucatini, I have prepared mine with gluten-free casarecce, but feel free to use any chunky pasta shape to soak up the stunning sauce. This is a rich and comforting family dish that will leave your house smelling amazing.

Season the chicken with salt and pepper.

Heat the olive oil in a large saucepan over medium–high heat. Add the chicken and sear, turning occasionally, for 10 minutes until browned all over. Set the chicken aside in a bowl.

Reduce the heat to low, add the onion and a generous pinch of salt to the pan and sauté, stirring occasionally, for 5 minutes to soften. Stir in the garlic, tomato paste, bay leaves, thyme, oregano, cinnamon, allspice, cloves and a pinch of black pepper and sauté for 2 minutes.

Deglaze the pan with the red wine, stirring to release any caramelised bits caught on the base, and simmer for 2–3 minutes until reduced by half. Tip in the tomatoes and 125 ml (½ cup) of water and stir to combine. Return the chicken and resting juices to the pan, cover and simmer for 30 minutes. Uncover the pan and simmer for another 30 minutes to thicken the sauce. Taste and adjust the seasoning with extra salt or pepper if required.

When the chicken is almost ready, cook the pasta according to the packet directions until al dente. Drain, then tip the pasta directly into the sauce (save some pasta water in case you need it to thin out the sauce). Gently stir to combine. Scatter on the parsley and cheese (if using) and serve.

NOTE
— You can replace the marylands with six skinless chicken thighs if preferred.

Prawn Saganaki with Spaghetti

80 ml (⅓ cup) extra-virgin olive oil, plus extra for drizzling

1 large onion, finely chopped

sea salt flakes and freshly ground black pepper

3 garlic cloves, finely chopped

½–1 long red chilli, halved lengthways, deseeded and finely sliced

2 tablespoons tomato paste

125 ml (½ cup) ouzo (see Notes)

400 g can crushed tomatoes

½ teaspoon dried oregano

320 g gluten-free spaghetti

16 large raw prawns, peeled and deveined, tails intact

100 g Greek feta, crumbled (optional)

handful of flat-leaf parsley leaves, finely chopped

DFO, GF | **SERVES 4**

Whenever I visit the Greek islands, the one summery dish I love to end my day with is prawn saganaki. What's not to love about garlicky prawns simmered in a rich tomato sauce oozing with melted feta? Prawn saganaki is most commonly served in tavernas as an appetiser in a small cast-iron vessel, but I absolutely love it tossed through spaghetti, so the pasta strands soak up the delicious sauce. This express pasta dish can be made in less than 20 minutes, perfect for your own mouthwatering Greek island dinner at home.

Fill a large saucepan with salted water and bring to the boil in preparation for the pasta.

Heat the olive oil in a large frying pan over low heat. Add the onion and a pinch of salt and sauté, stirring occasionally, for 8 minutes to soften. Stir in the garlic, chilli and tomato paste and cook for another minute. Pour in the ouzo and simmer for 2–3 minutes or until reduced by half. Add the crushed tomatoes, oregano and a pinch of salt and pepper. Cover and simmer for 10 minutes to thicken the sauce.

While the sauce is simmering, cook the spaghetti according to the packet directions until almost al dente.

Add the prawns to the sauce, sprinkle on some salt and cook for a minute until they are just opaque. A minute before the spaghetti is ready, transfer the pasta directly into the sauce with tongs, dragging along some of the starchy pasta water. Gently toss to combine, and simmer for 1 minute to complete cooking the prawns (if you need to thin out the sauce, add more pasta water). Remove from the heat. Scatter on the feta (if using) and the parsley, season with a little more pepper and drizzle on some extra olive oil. Serve immediately.

NOTES

— The ouzo adds some beautiful anise notes in the background, but feel free to use white wine if you prefer.

— Be careful not to overcook your prawns or they will turn rubbery. They need to simmer for only 3 minutes.

Spaghetti Vongole with Zucchini & Lemon

125 ml (½ cup) extra-virgin olive oil

½ long red chilli, halved lengthways, deseeded and finely sliced

3 garlic cloves, finely sliced

2 large zucchini, spiralised or sliced into thin strips

sea salt flakes and freshly ground black pepper

350 g gluten-free spaghetti

125 ml (½ cup) white wine

1 kg vongole (clams), purged

1 teaspoon finely grated lemon zest

juice of ½ lemon

large handful of flat-leaf parsley leaves, finely chopped

DF, GF | **SERVES 4**

When I was studying at university, I travelled through Italy, eating copious amounts of pasta – and spaghetti vongole was one of my favourites. I have a distinct memory of a version with thin ribbons of zucchini swirled through it that I enjoyed in a small, no-frills trattoria in Rome. The sweetness of the zucchini paired beautifully with the salty vongole swimming in the white wine broth. It was so memorable, I had to recreate it at home.

Don't be alarmed by the volume of zucchini in the pan, it will collapse quite a bit during cooking. I find it best to spiralise the zucchini into strands, so they bend and twirl like spaghetti; if you don't own a spiraliser, thin strips still work.

Fill a large saucepan with salted water and bring to the boil in preparation for the pasta.

Heat the olive oil in a large frying pan over medium heat and add the chilli, garlic, zucchini and a generous pinch of salt. Cook, stirring regularly, for 10 minutes or until the zucchini is golden and collapsed.

Halfway through cooking the zucchini, add the spaghetti to the boiling salted water and cook according to the packet directions until almost al dente.

Add the white wine, vongole, lemon zest and 80 ml (⅓ cup) of the starchy pasta water to the zucchini. Cover the pan and cook for 3–4 minutes or until the vongole open (discard any unopened ones).

Using tongs, drag the spaghetti into the frying pan along with some of the starchy pasta water. Toss to combine and cook for another minute. Take off the heat, squeeze in the lemon juice and sprinkle on the parsley. Serve with a grinding of black pepper.

Rigatoni with Creamy Broccolini Pesto

2 bunches of broccolini, trimmed

320 g gluten-free rigatoni

large handful of basil leaves, plus extra to serve

2 garlic cloves, bashed and peeled

40 g (¼ cup) pine nuts, toasted

65 g (¾ cup) finely grated pecorino or parmigiano reggiano, plus extra to serve

125 ml (½ cup) extra-virgin olive oil

pinch of sea salt flakes and freshly ground black pepper

DFO, GF, V, VGO | SERVES 4

As a mum I'm constantly looking for ways to get my kids to eat more greens. If I can disguise most of them, I'm halfway there, and that is why I rely on this deliciously creamy (yet without a drop of cream) pasta recipe. The blanched broccolini stems are blitzed into the pesto for a vibrant punch of green, and the simple addition of starchy pasta water magically transforms the pesto into a smooth creamy sauce. I have separated the florets from the broccolini stalks for added texture and bite, but if you prefer to completely disguise the veggies, just add all the broccolini to the pesto sauce. A healthy serve of veggies in every pasta bowl – Mum win!

Fill a large saucepan with salted water and bring to the boil in preparation for the pasta.

Separate the broccolini florets and stalks by cutting two-thirds of the way up each stalk. Add the broccolini stalks to the simmering water and cook for 2 minutes. Remove the stalks with tongs and transfer directly to a food processor.

Using the same water, cook the pasta according to the packet directions until almost al dente.

While the pasta cooks, add the basil, garlic, pine nuts, cheese, olive oil and salt and pepper to the broccolini in the food processor, then blitz to combine. With the motor running, slowly pour in 60 ml (¼ cup) of the starchy pasta water and process until a creamy sauce forms (if the sauce is too thick, add more water). Taste and adjust the seasoning as required.

In the last 2 minutes of cooking time for the pasta, add the broccolini florets to the pasta water. Drain the pasta and florets in a large colander and return to the empty pan. Pour on the broccolini pesto and toss to combine. Serve with a grinding of pepper and a sprinkle of extra cheese and basil leaves.

VARIATION

—For a delicious dairy-free version, simply omit the cheese.

Pasta Al Forno
Baked Pasta

3 tablespoons extra-virgin olive oil

1 onion, finely chopped

1 carrot, finely chopped

1 celery stalk, finely chopped

sea salt flakes and freshly ground black pepper

2 garlic cloves, finely chopped

2 tablespoons tomato paste

250 g pork mince

250 g beef mince

2 x 400 g cans crushed tomatoes

125 ml (½ cup) red wine

1 teaspoon dried oregano

pinch of grated nutmeg

400 g gluten-free paccheri (see Note)

handful of basil leaves

200 g mozzarella, coarsely grated

80 g pecorino or parmigiano reggiano, finely grated

GF | **SERVES 6**

Pasta al forno is a rustic Italian baked pasta dish that translates to 'pasta from the oven'. Unlike lasagne and pastitsio, my pasta al forno is covered with a simple layer of stretchy mozzarella and sharp pecorino for a golden, crunchy top, which is simpler to prepare than bechamel but just as delicious. Every Italian family has their own version of this recipe; some include sausage, peas, salami or boiled eggs, but all feature a rich tomato sauce, gooey cheese and crunchy edges. Perfect family comfort food.

Heat the olive oil in a large saucepan over medium–low heat, add the onion, carrot, celery and a pinch of salt and sauté for 10 minutes or until softened. Stir in the garlic and tomato paste and cook, stirring continuously, for another minute.

Add the minces to the pan and brown for 2–3 minutes, breaking it up with a wooden spoon. Add the crushed tomatoes, red wine, oregano and nutmeg and season with salt and pepper. Cover and simmer over low heat for 1 hour or until the sauce is thick and rich.

Preheat the oven to 200°C (fan-forced) and bring a large saucepan of salted water to the boil. Cook the pasta according to the packet directions until al dente. Transfer the pasta directly to the sauce with a slotted spoon and toss to combine.

Grease a 25 cm × 30 cm baking dish. Layer half the saucy pasta into the dish. Scatter on a few basil leaves and half the cheese. Repeat the layers, finishing with the cheese. Bake for 20 minutes or until the top is golden and crispy. Serve with a grinding of pepper.

NOTE

— If you can't find paccheri, you can replace it with a chunky rigatoni.

Silverbeet & Ricotta Cannelloni

3 tablespoons extra-virgin olive oil

1 bunch of silverbeet, leaves shredded

350 g fresh ricotta, well drained

1 egg, lightly whisked

¼ teaspoon grated nutmeg

75 g (¾ cup) grated parmigiano reggiano or pecorino

sea salt flakes and freshly ground black pepper

1 onion, finely chopped

handful of basil, stems finely chopped and leaves shredded

1 garlic clove, finely chopped

2 x 400 g cans crushed tomatoes

16 gluten-free cannelloni shells

150 g (1 cup) coarsely grated mozzarella

chopped flat-leaf parsley leaves, to serve (optional)

GF, V | SERVES 4–6

Silverbeet has always been my favourite leafy green to cook with. I love its mild sweet flavour and waxy texture in rustic winter soups, spanakopita and bean stews. Native to the Mediterranean, it is used extensively in the region due to its year-round availability, versatility, excellent nutritional profile and warming mellow taste. Silverbeet and ricotta cannelloni, one of the first recipes I started cooking when I moved out of home, holds many treasured memories as it was my go-to dinner party recipe. I've certainly extended my repertoire since then, but it's a comforting classic I always come back to.

Preheat the oven to 200°C (fan-forced).

Heat 1 tablespoon of the olive oil in a large frying pan over medium heat. Add the silverbeet and sauté for 5 minutes until wilted. Set aside to cool.

Combine the ricotta, egg, nutmeg and 50 g (½ cup) of the parmigiano or pecorino in a bowl. Using your hands, squeeze out the moisture from the wilted silverbeet and add to the bowl. Season with salt and pepper and mix well.

Heat the remaining oil in a frying pan over low heat. Add the onion, basil stems and a pinch of salt and cook, stirring occasionally, for 5 minutes to soften. Stir in the garlic and cook for another 30 seconds. Add the tomatoes and a pinch of salt and pepper. Simmer for 20 minutes to reduce. Remove from the heat and stir through the basil leaves.

Spread ½ cup of the tomato sauce over the base of a roughly 20 cm × 30 cm baking dish. Fill the cannelloni shells with the ricotta mixture using a piping bag or long spoon. Arrange the shells in the dish, then pour on the remaining tomato sauce. Sprinkle on the remaining parmigiano or pecorino and the mozzarella. Cover the dish with foil and bake for 25 minutes. Remove the foil and bake, uncovered, for 10 minutes or until golden. Allow to rest for a few minutes, then sprinkle on a little parsley (if using) and serve.

NOTE

— Do not discard your silverbeet stalks. Chop them up and simmer with other vegetable trimmings – like celery leaves, carrot peel and onion trimmings – to make a vegetable stock.

Duck Ragu with Pappardelle

4 duck marylands

sea salt flakes and freshly ground black pepper

1 onion, finely chopped

1 large carrot, finely chopped

1 celery stalk, finely chopped

3 garlic cloves, chopped

1 tablespoon roughly chopped rosemary leaves

2 tablespoons thyme leaves

1 cinnamon stick

pinch of grated nutmeg

250 ml (1 cup) dry white wine

500 ml (2 cups) Chicken Stock (page 206)

400 g gluten-free pappardelle

finely chopped flat-leaf parsley leaves, to serve

finely grated pecorino, to serve (optional)

DFO, GF | SERVES 4

As much as I love tomatoes in a rich, red ragu, sometimes I feel like something less bold and acidic, so I'll braise my meat in a delicate white wine sauce. Duck ragu may sound intimidating or too luxurious but it really is very simple to prepare. The gamey duck in this Venetian ragu is perfumed with piney rosemary, thyme, nutmeg and sweet cinnamon for a well-rounded flavour. Like all slow-cooked pasta sauces, the flavours intensify overnight, so it is even better the next day.

Season the duck with salt and pepper and place in a heavy-based saucepan. Turn the heat to medium and cook for 8 minutes to slowly render the fat, turning halfway through. Remove the duck from the pan and set aside.

Add the onion, carrot, celery and a pinch of salt to the fat remaining in the pan, reduce the heat to low and sauté, stirring occasionally, for 8 minutes to soften. Add the garlic, rosemary, thyme, cinnamon and nutmeg and cook for another 30 seconds.

Deglaze the pan with the white wine, stirring to release any caramelised bits caught on the base, and simmer for 2–3 minutes until reduced by half. Add the stock and bring to a simmer. Return the duck and the resting juices to the pan, cover and gently simmer for 1 hour. Remove the lid and simmer, uncovered, for 30 minutes or until the sauce is thickened and the duck is tender.

When the sauce is almost ready, cook the pasta according to the packet directions until al dente.

Remove the duck from the pan, shred the meat off the bone and return the shredded meat to the pan. Using tongs, directly transfer the pasta to the ragu, dragging along some of the starchy pasta water. Gently toss to combine (and add more pasta water if required to loosen the sauce). Scatter with parsley and pecorino (if using) and serve.

Penne with Charred Capsicum & Sun-dried Tomato Sauce

3 red bullhorn capsicums, tops trimmed, halved lengthways and deseeded

320 g gluten-free penne

75 g (½ cup) sun-dried tomatoes

2 tablespoons almonds, toasted and chopped, plus extra to serve

1 garlic clove, bashed and peeled

125 ml (½ cup) extra-virgin olive oil

sea salt flakes and freshly ground black pepper

finely chopped flat-leaf parsley leaves, to serve

DF, GF, VG | **SERVES 4**

When red capsicums are charred, their natural sweetness is enhanced, taking on caramelised notes and a stunning velvety texture – the perfect base for a silky, robust pasta sauce. Blitz and combine with tangy sun-dried tomatoes and toasted almonds for a creamy sauce with a vibrant orange hue that is so delicious it can be enjoyed as a stand-alone dip. This deeply flavourful and luxurious vegan sauce requires only a handful of pantry ingredients. File under 'quick and easy'.

Preheat the oven grill to high.

Arrange the capsicum on a baking tray, skin-side up, and place under the hot grill. Cook for 10 minutes or until the skin is blistered and charred. Transfer the capsicum to a bowl and cover with plastic wrap (the trapped steam will help release the skin from the flesh). When the capsicum has cooled, peel away the skin and transfer the flesh to a food processor.

Bring a large saucepan of salted water to the boil and cook the pasta according to the packet directions until al dente.

While the pasta cooks, add the sun-dried tomatoes, almonds, garlic, olive oil and a good pinch of salt and pepper to the capsicum in the food processor. Blitz to form a creamy, vibrant orange sauce. Transfer the sauce to a frying pan and place over low heat.

When the pasta is ready, use a slotted spoon to transfer the penne directly to the sauce, dragging along some of the starchy pasta water. Toss to combine (add a splash more pasta water if needed to loosen the sauce). Scatter on some parsley and extra almonds, for added crunch, and add a grinding of black pepper to serve.

SEA

FOOD

Kakavia
Fisherman's Soup

3 tablespoons extra-virgin olive oil

1 onion, finely chopped

2 large carrots, sliced diagonally

2 celery stalks, sliced diagonally

sea salt flakes and freshly ground black pepper

1 tablespoon tomato paste

1 large all-purpose potato (such as sebago), peeled and cut into 3 cm cubes

2 tomatoes, grated, skin discarded

12 mussels, cleaned and debearded

juice of 1 small lemon

finely chopped flat-leaf parsley leaves and lemon wedges, to serve

FISH STOCK

1 whole snapper (roughly 1.4 kg), scaled, cleaned and cut into 3 pieces

2 garlic cloves, bashed and peeled

3 fresh bay leaves

pinch of saffron threads

2 teaspoons sea salt flakes

10 black peppercorns

DF, GF | SERVES 4

Kakavia is a soup Greek fishermen prepare on their boats to feed the crew using the day's catch. The name is derived from the 'kakavi', the tripod cooking pot ancient Greek fishermen used to cook the soup. Kakavia is similar to other Mediterranean fish stews like French bouillabaisse, Italian cacciucco, Spanish zarzuela and Portuguese caldeirada. The aim is to use the freshest seafood possible, but you can be quite flexible with the ingredients, which are generally a combination of fish, shellfish, vegetables, saffron and a tomato broth. I love the combination of delicate sweet snapper and mussels for that fresh ocean flavour; feel free to add vongole (clams), pipis or prawns, if you wish.

To make the fish stock, place the snapper in a stockpot and add 1.5 litres of water, the garlic, bay leaves, saffron, salt and peppercorns. Cover and simmer over low heat for 30 minutes. Remove the snapper to a shallow bowl and strain the murky stock into a large bowl, discarding the solids.

Heat the olive oil in a large saucepan over low heat. Add the onion, carrot, celery and a pinch of salt and sauté, stirring occasionally, for 10 minutes to soften the vegetables. Stir in the tomato paste and cook for 1 minute. Add the potato, tomato and strained fish stock and bring to the boil. Reduce the heat to low, cover and simmer for 8 minutes. Add the mussels and simmer for 4–5 minutes or until they have opened (discard any that do not open). Using a slotted spoon, scoop out 1–2 cups of vegetables and blitz in a food processor to form a puree (the more vegetables in your puree the thicker your soup will be). Return the puree to the pan and stir to combine and add body to the soup. Take off the heat and squeeze in the lemon juice. Taste and adjust the seasoning with more salt as required.

Remove the snapper flesh from the bones and divide equally among serving bowls. Pour in the soup, season with a little black pepper, scatter on some parsley and serve with lemon wedges.

NOTE

— For a more flavoursome fish stock, ask your fishmonger for extra fish heads and bones (anything but salmon) to add to the pot when simmering the snapper.

Slow-roasted Salmon with Salsa Verde

1 kg salmon or trout fillet, skin and bones removed (see Note)

2 tablespoons extra-virgin olive oil

2 teaspoons sea salt flakes

pinch of freshly ground black pepper

lemon wedges, to serve

SALSA VERDE

large handful of flat-leaf parsley leaves, plus extra to serve

large handful of basil leaves, plus extra to serve

1 garlic clove, bashed and peeled

2 teaspoons capers, drained

3 anchovy fillets

juice of 1 small lemon

125 ml (½ cup) extra-virgin olive oil

sea salt flakes and freshly ground black pepper

DF, GF | SERVES 4–6

Most home cooks wouldn't associate slow roasting with seafood but once you take it low and slow with a fillet of salmon or trout you will never revert to a quick blast of heat again. Slow cooking gradually renders the fat, so the fish cooks more evenly, producing a silky, melt-in-your-mouth texture. Paired with a bright, zesty salsa verde and you have an elegant, healthy, single piece of protein to feed an entire family.

Preheat the oven to 120°C (fan-forced).

Place the salmon or trout fillet in a deep baking tray, drizzle on the olive oil and season all sides with the salt and pepper. Bake for 40 minutes, basting the fish with the tray juices halfway through cooking. Transfer the fish to a platter and drizzle on the tray juices.

Meanwhile, to make the salsa verde, place the parsley, basil, garlic, capers and anchovy fillets in a food processor and blitz to combine. With the motor running, drizzle in the lemon juice and olive oil and process until combined. Taste and adjust the seasoning as required.

Drizzle the salsa verde over the fish, scatter with extra parsley and basil leaves and serve with lemon wedges.

NOTE

—When cooking a large piece of protein like this, to help it cook more evenly, take it out of the fridge an hour prior to cooking to bring it to room temperature.

Bourdeto
Tomato-poached Fish

80 ml (⅓ cup) extra-virgin olive oil

1 onion, finely chopped

sea salt flakes and freshly ground black pepper

3 garlic cloves, finely chopped

1 teaspoon paprika

pinch of chilli flakes (optional)

125 ml (½ cup) dry white wine

200 g canned crushed tomatoes

400 g chat potatoes, halved

10 kalamata olives

600 g cod fillets (or other firm white fish, such as perch or coral trout), skin and bones removed, cut into 6 cm pieces

squeeze of lemon juice and finely chopped flat-leaf parsley leaves, to serve

DF, GF | **SERVES 4–6**

Bourdeto is a spiced tomato, poached fish dish native to Corfu. The flavours build up very quickly – sauté onion, layer in some spice, add wine with potatoes and salty olives and let everything gently simmer away. Nestle your fish fillets in the pan for the last 5 minutes and you have a beautiful, nourishing one-pan dinner in less than 40 minutes. It is traditionally prepared with scorpion fish (a species not readily available in Australia) but you can make it with cod or another firm white fish.

Heat the olive oil in a frying pan over low heat, add the onion and a pinch of salt and cook, stirring occasionally, for 5 minutes to soften. Stir in the garlic, paprika and chilli flakes (if using) and cook for another 30 seconds.

Deglaze the pan with the white wine, stirring to release any caramelised bits caught on the base, and simmer for 2 minutes or until reduced by half. Add the tomatoes, potato, olives, 250 ml (1 cup) of water and a pinch of black pepper. Bring to a simmer, cover and cook, stirring occasionally, for 25–30 minutes or until the potato is tender.

Season the fish with salt and pepper and nestle the fillets in the tomato sauce. Cover and poach the fish for 5 minutes or until just cooked through. Remove from the heat. Squeeze in the lemon juice, scatter with parsley and serve.

Oktapodi Ksidato
Maria's Octopus with Oregano Vinaigrette

1 kg large octopus, cleaned and skin removed (see Note)

125 ml (½ cup) red wine vinegar

3 fresh bay leaves

2 teaspoons sea salt flakes, plus extra if needed

1 red bullhorn capsicum, halved lengthways, deseeded, cut into thin half rounds

1 tablespoon capers, drained

OREGANO VINAIGRETTE

125 ml (½ cup) extra-virgin olive oil

3 tablespoons red wine vinegar

2 garlic cloves, crushed

1 teaspoon dried oregano

pinch of freshly ground white pepper, plus extra if needed

DF, GF | **SERVES 4–6**

Every yiayia has a signature dish: the one defining recipe that stands out as 'best in class'. Octopus ksidato is that dish for my mother-in-law Maria. She learned how to cook perfect octopus growing up on the beautiful Ionian island of Kefalonia, where fresh seafood is abundant. My kids devour Yiayia's octopus every time she brings it over, so I knew it was a must for this book.

'Ksidi' (vinegar in Greek) is the prominent flavour in this dish. Vinegar not only flavours the octopus, it also tenderises the meat by dissolving the tough connective tissue. My mother-in-law taught me to peel the octopus prior to cooking as the skin can become quite gelatinous once boiled (this is not an issue if you are finishing your octopus on a chargrill because these mushy bits crisp up beautifully). Toss the octopus with salty capers and slivers of capsicum and bathe in a zesty olive oil vinaigrette for a bright, acidic finish. This is Kefalonian summer on a plate.

Place the octopus in a saucepan, then add the vinegar, bay leaves, salt and 1 litre of water. Bring to the boil, reduce the heat to low, cover and simmer for 40 minutes or until the octopus is tender when pierced with a fork. (Be careful not to overcook the octopus or it will turn mushy.) Remove the octopus from the pan and set aside to cool for 10 minutes.

Cut the tentacles into bite-sized pieces, place in a bowl and add the capsicum and capers.

Whisk the oregano vinaigrette ingredients together and pour over the octopus. Toss to combine, taste and add more salt or white pepper, if required. Set aside to marinate for 30 minutes before serving.

NOTE

— To remove the octopus skin, take an uncooked whole, cleaned octopus and separate a small piece of skin and flesh at the head with your fingers. Lift the skin and peel it back in one piece (the suckers will remain intact). Most of the skin should come away easily. You will probably need to work in sections, so repeat the process a few times.

Baked Lemon Snapper with Green Olives & Potato

1 x 1.6 kg whole snapper, scaled and cleaned (see Notes)

80 ml (⅓ cup) extra-virgin olive oil

sea salt flakes and freshly ground black pepper

2 pinches of dried oregano

2 garlic cloves, finely sliced

1 lemon, finely sliced

500 g chat potatoes, cut in half

90 g (½ cup) green Sicilian olives

DF, GF | **SERVES 4**

Snapper is my favourite fish to cook whole because of its slightly sweet, delicate, juicy flesh and crispy skin. Not only does a whole piece of fish look super impressive as a dinner-table centrepiece, it requires minimal effort and only a handful of pantry staples. For classic Mediterranean flavours, simply season your fish with salt, pepper, oregano and olive oil and sit it on a bed of finely sliced lemon. When roasted, the lemon magically caramelises, releasing sweetness into the tray juices – delicious spooned over your moist, flaky fish.

Preheat the oven to 200°C (fan-forced).

Thoroughly dry the fish with paper towel. Brush both sides of the skin with half the olive oil and season the skin and cavity with a generous pinch of salt, pepper and oregano. Lightly score three diagonal incisions on one side of the fish, then press the garlic slices into the incisions. Place three lemon slices in the fish cavity.

Arrange the remaining lemon slices in the centre of a large deep baking tray and place the fish on top. Scatter the potato around the fish, drizzle the remaining oil over them, season with salt and another pinch of oregano and scatter in the green olives. Bake, turning the potato halfway through cooking, for 30 minutes or until the fish is opaque when flaked with a fork and the potato is crispy. Spoon the tray juices and caramelised lemon over the fish and serve.

NOTES

— Your fishmonger can scale, gut and clean a whole fish for you so half the work is already done.

— A whole snapper will yield about 50 per cent meat once the bones are discarded: a 1.6 kg snapper will yield 800 g total meat or 200 g per person. If you are cooking for two, use an 800 g whole fish instead and reduce the baking time by 10 minutes.

Crispy Barramundi with Tahini Sauce & Watercress–Pomegranate Salad

4 x 180 g barramundi fillets,
bones removed

3 tablespoons extra-virgin olive oil

2 teaspoons sea salt flakes

pinch of freshly ground
black pepper

TAHINI SAUCE

3 tablespoons tahini

3 tablespoons freshly squeezed
lemon juice

1 garlic clove, crushed

1 teaspoon honey

pinch of sea salt flakes and
freshly ground black pepper

WATERCRESS–POMEGRANATE
SALAD

1 bunch of watercress sprigs

handful of flat-leaf parsley leaves,
roughly chopped

2 tablespoons pomegranate seeds

2 tablespoons extra-virgin olive oil

1 teaspoon sumac

1 tablespoon freshly squeezed
lemon juice

DF, GF | **SERVES 4**

Tahini with fish is a common pairing in Middle Eastern countries. The creaminess of tahini is a much healthier – and, in my opinion, much tastier – alternative to butter, and it works brilliantly. Crispy pan-seared barramundi with its flaky delicate flesh is the perfect partner to tahini's creaminess and is super quick to prepare. Sumac-kissed watercress accompanied by antioxidant-rich pomegranate seeds adds freshness and vibrancy to a clean and healthy express dinner.

Whisk the tahini sauce ingredients in a bowl. Slowly drizzle in a little cold water while whisking to create a thick, smooth puree. Set aside.

Thoroughly pat the skin on the fish dry to remove any moisture (dry skin equals crispy fish). Drizzle 2 tablespoons of the olive oil over both sides of the fish and season with the salt and pepper. Massage the seasoning all over the fish.

Heat the remaining oil in a large frying pan over medium–high heat. Place the fish, skin-side down, in the pan and use a spatula to press down on it for 20 seconds (this creates strong contact between the skin and the hot pan and prevents the fish from curling up). Cook for 4–5 minutes until crispy. Flip the fish over and cook for another 2 minutes. Transfer the fish to a plate and rest in a warm place for a few minutes.

Meanwhile, to make the watercress–pomegranate salad, combine the watercress, parsley and pomegranate seeds in a bowl. Whisk together the olive oil, sumac, lemon juice and a pinch of salt and pepper to make a dressing. Drizzle the dressing over the salad and toss to combine.

To serve, divide the tahini sauce and salad among serving plates and place the fish on top.

Chicken Shawarma

1 kg skinless chicken thigh fillets

Toum (page 209), gluten-free Pita Bread (page 24) and lemon wedges, to serve

GARLICKY MARINADE

4 large garlic cloves, finely grated

3 teaspoons ground coriander

3 teaspoons ground cumin

3 teaspoons sea salt flakes

1 teaspoon paprika

1 teaspoon allspice

½ teaspoon cayenne pepper (add more for extra spice)

¼ teaspoon freshly ground black pepper

3 tablespoons extra-virgin olive oil

2 tablespoons freshly squeezed lemon juice

DF, GF | SERVES 4–6

When I was at university, a chicken shawarma wrap slathered in garlicky toum was one of my favourite late-night street foods. The exotic spices wafted from the kebab shop luring me in and the incredible taste of heavily spiced meat was hard to match. Fast forward 20 years and I make shawarma regularly for dinner as it requires minimum effort for explosive flavour. Simply throw a few Middle Eastern pantry spices in a bowl, add the chicken and allow the magic of the fragrant marinade to work overnight. The next day you are rewarded with a spice flavour bomb. You can serve shawarma with a vibrant fresh salad like tabbouleh (page 47).

Lightly score the thick part of the chicken thighs with a couple of incisions to help the meat cook evenly.

Combine the garlicky marinade ingredients in a large non-reactive bowl. Add the chicken and massage the marinade into the flesh. Cover the bowl and refrigerate overnight (if you are rushed for time, you can marinate the chicken for 1 hour; longer marination equals more flavour).

Remove the chicken from the fridge 30 minutes before cooking and bring to room temperature. Heat a chargrill pan or barbecue grill plate until very hot. Add the chicken and cook for 4–5 minutes until nicely charred. Turn and cook for another 2 minutes or until cooked through. Rest the chicken for 4 minutes before thickly slicing. Serve with toum, pita bread and lemon wedges.

NOTE

—Chicken thigh fillets are best for this dish because they have more fat, giving you juicy, tender meat, but you can also use chicken breast fillets if you prefer.

Apricot Chicken Tagine

800 g skinless chicken thigh fillets

1 tablespoon extra-virgin olive oil

2 red onions, finely sliced

sea salt flakes and freshly ground black pepper

90 g (½ cup) dried apricots

1 cinnamon stick

3 whole cloves

juice of 1 small lemon

handful of almonds, toasted and roughly chopped (optional)

cooked quinoa (see page 160), to serve

GINGER MARINADE

5 garlic cloves, bashed and peeled

3 cm piece of ginger, grated

2 teaspoons sea salt flakes

2 teaspoons ground cumin

2 teaspoons smoked paprika

1 teaspoon ground cinnamon

1 teaspoon ground turmeric

¼ teaspoon freshly ground black pepper

small bunch of coriander, stems and roots roughly chopped, leaves reserved to serve

3 tablespoons extra-virgin olive oil

DF, GF | SERVES 4–6

Moroccan tagines are renowned for their delicious sweet and savoury flavours and contrasting textures. This warming tagine combines subtle sweetness from dried apricots, heat from aromatic spices and crunch from toasted almonds, with meltingly tender chicken in a syrupy stock.

You don't need to own a clay cone-shaped tagine to prepare this; a large heavy-based casserole dish will work just fine. Quite often North African stews call for preserved lemons, but my kids find their flavour too astringent, so I add a squeeze of lemon juice for acidity and brightness instead.

Place the ginger marinade ingredients in a food processor and blitz to form a paste.

Combine the chicken and marinade in a large bowl, cover and marinate in the fridge for 1 hour or, even better, overnight (if you are rushed for time, you can skip the marination time, but the flavour won't be as intense).

Heat the olive oil in a tagine or flameproof casserole dish over medium-high heat. Add the chicken in batches and cook for 2–3 minutes on each side until nicely browned. Remove and set aside. Reduce the heat to low, add the onion and a pinch of salt and cook for 5 minutes to soften. Stir in 250 ml (1 cup) of water, scraping any caramelised bits from the base of the dish. Add the apricots, cinnamon and cloves. Return the chicken and resting juices to the dish, cover and simmer for 30 minutes. Remove from the heat and squeeze in the lemon juice. Taste and adjust the seasoning as required. Add a grinding of black pepper, top with the toasted almonds (if using) and reserved coriander leaves and serve with cooked quinoa.

Sage & Pecorino-crumbed Chicken

2 chicken breast fillets

30 g (¼ cup) tapioca flour

2 eggs, lightly whisked

70 g (1 cup) gluten-free dried breadcrumbs

45 g (½ cup) finely grated pecorino

1 teaspoon paprika

1 teaspoon sea salt flakes, plus extra to serve

pinch of freshly ground black pepper

15 g (⅓ cup) finely chopped sage leaves

light olive oil, for shallow-frying

lemon halves, to serve

GF | **SERVES 4**

The pronounced peppery sage, sharp pecorino and smoky paprika work in harmony in this delicious, full-flavoured crumb. Dusting the chicken with tapioca flour helps adhere the crumb to the tender meat, so, for an extra crunchy crust, ensure you don't skip this step. Depending on how much oil you like to use, you can fry, bake or air-fry your crumbed chicken. For added variety, feel free to swap the chicken for veal or pork and the pecorino for parmigiano reggiano.

Place a chicken breast fillet on a chopping board. Firmly press down on the breast with the palm of your hand and slice horizontally to create two thin fillets (you can cut the chicken into smaller strips if you wish). Gently bash the thicker parts with your fist to flatten. Repeat with the remaining chicken breast.

Set up a crumbing station with three shallow bowls: one for the tapioca flour, one for the whisked egg and in the third combine the breadcrumbs, pecorino, paprika, salt, pepper and sage to form a crumb mixture.

Dust the chicken with the tapioca flour, shaking off the excess. Dip in the egg, then firmly press into the crumb mixture.

To fry, heat enough olive oil for shallow-frying in a large, deep frying pan until it reaches 180°C on a kitchen thermometer (or until a cube of gluten-free bread dropped in the hot oil browns in 15 seconds). Working in batches, add the chicken and fry for 5 minutes, turning halfway through cooking, until evenly browned and cooked through. Drain on a wire rack. Sprinkle with salt and serve with lemon halves for squeezing.

NOTES

— To air-fry the chicken, spray both sides of the meat with olive oil spray. Preheat the air-fryer for 3 minutes at 200°C. Place the chicken on the rack and cook for 10 minutes, turning halfway through cooking.

— To bake the chicken, preheat the oven to 220°C (fan-forced). Drizzle both sides of the chicken with olive oil (or use olive oil spray if you prefer), place on a baking tray and bake for 12–15 minutes or until golden and cooked through.

Souvlakia
Chicken Skewers

800 g chicken breast fillets or skinless thigh fillets, cut into 3 cm cubes

Tzatziki (page 208), Greek salad and gluten-free Pita Bread (page 24), to serve

LEMON–GARLIC MARINADE

3 tablespoons extra-virgin olive oil

2 tablespoons freshly squeezed lemon juice, plus extra to serve

3 garlic cloves, crushed

1 tablespoon sea salt flakes

1 tablespoon dried oregano

2 teaspoons dijon mustard

pinch of freshly ground black pepper

GF | SERVES 4–6

Whenever I host a barbecue at my house the chicken souvlakia always disappear first – and with good reason. They are easy to eat, the lemon, garlic and oregano marinade tastes delicious and keeps the meat moist, and everyone loves chicken.

Chicken souvlakia can be made with breast or thigh, it is personal preference. Breast is leaner; thigh is fattier and juicier. I love both.

Place the lemon–garlic marinade ingredients in a large non-reactive bowl and mix well. Add the chicken and massage the marinade into the meat. Thread the chicken onto metal skewers (roughly 100 g meat per skewer). Place on a plate, cover and marinate in the fridge for a few hours or, even better, overnight.

Heat a chargrill pan over high heat until smoking hot. Cook the souvlakia, turning regularly, for 8 minutes until browned all over. Remove from the pan, rest and squeeze over some extra lemon juice. Serve with tzatziki, salad and pita bread.

Keftedes
Chicken Meatballs

light olive oil, for shallow-frying

Tzatziki (page 208) and
lemon wedges, to serve

CHICKEN MEATBALLS

500 g chicken mince

1 all-purpose potato (such as
sebago), peeled and very finely
grated, excess moisture
squeezed out

1 small red onion, grated, excess
moisture squeezed out

2 garlic cloves, finely grated

1 egg

handful of flat-leaf parsley leaves,
finely chopped, plus extra sprigs
to serve

handful of mint leaves, finely
chopped, plus extra sprigs to serve

1 teaspoon finely grated lemon zest

1 teaspoon dried oregano

2 teaspoons ground cumin

generous pinch of sea salt flakes
and freshly ground black pepper

GF | SERVES 4–6

These gorgeously juicy chicken meatballs taste lighter and sweeter than their beef counterparts – and this is why kids are obsessed with them. Meatballs require a starchy component to keep them light and fluffy, so I have swapped out breadcrumbs with finely grated potato to produce the lightest, fluffiest meatball you will ever taste. Beautifully seasoned with fresh herbs, lemon zest, dried oregano and cumin, a squeeze of lemon and a good smear of creamy tzatziki are all you need to finish.

Combine the chicken meatball ingredients in a large non-reactive bowl and mix well by hand. Refrigerate for 30 minutes to firm up, then roll the mixture into 16 balls. (I find it helpful to wet or oil my hands prior to rolling to stop the mince sticking to my fingers.)

Heat enough olive oil for shallow-frying in a large, deep frying pan until it reaches 180°C on a kitchen thermometer (or until a cube of gluten-free bread dropped in the hot oil browns in 15 seconds). Add the meatballs in batches and fry, turning regularly, for 5 minutes or until browned all over. Remove from the pan and drain on paper towel. Serve with tzatziki, lemon wedges and extra herbs.

NOTE
—These meatballs freeze really well, so you might like to double the batch, then portion and freeze your uncooked meatballs for up to 2 months. Thaw completely before cooking.

Stifado
Rabbit & Onion Stew

1 rabbit (about 1 kg), cut into 8 pieces

sea salt flakes and freshly ground black pepper

125 ml (½ cup) extra-virgin olive oil

500 g pickling onions, peeled

5 garlic cloves, finely sliced

2 tablespoons tomato paste

250 ml (1 cup) red wine

2 tablespoons honey

3 fresh bay leaves

2 cinnamon sticks

½ teaspoon ground allspice

5 whole cloves

2 tablespoons balsamic vinegar

200 g canned crushed tomatoes

DF, GF | SERVES 4–6

Stifado is a mouthwatering slow-cooked Greek stew made with rabbit or beef and loads of sweet brown onions, aromatic spices, red wine and tomato. The caramelised onions release their sugars in the oven, resulting in the most intensely flavoured rich, thick sauce for braising the rabbit. This winter warmer is very easy to prepare – simply sear the meat, throw in the spices and liquids and forget about it as it slowly cooks, perfuming the kitchen with the most amazing aroma. Serve with rice, potatoes or crusty gluten-free bread.

Preheat the oven to 160°C (fan-forced).

Season the rabbit with salt and pepper. Heat 2 tablespoons of the olive oil in a large flameproof casserole dish over medium heat. Add the rabbit in batches and sear for 8 minutes or until browned all over. Remove and set aside.

Heat the remaining oil in the dish, add the onions and sauté, stirring occasionally, for 3 minutes or until golden. Stir in the garlic and tomato paste and cook for 30 seconds. Deglaze the dish with the red wine, stirring to release any caramelised bits caught on the base. Add the remaining ingredients, along with 125 ml (½ cup) of water and a pinch of salt and pepper. Stir to combine, then return the rabbit and the resting juices to the dish. Cover and transfer to the oven to braise for 1½ hours. Turn the rabbit pieces and continue to braise, uncovered if the sauce needs further reducing, for 30 minutes or until the rabbit is tender and the sauce has thickened. Taste and adjust the seasoning as required.

VARIATION

— The rabbit can be replaced with 1 kg chuck steak, cut into large chunks. Beef will require a longer cooking time, so braise in the oven for 2½–3 hours or until fork tender.

Porchetta
Roast Pork with Sage & Fennel

1 tablespoon fennel seeds

1 teaspoon black peppercorns

1 teaspoon sea salt flakes,
plus extra to season

4 garlic cloves, bashed and peeled

3 tablespoons chopped
sage leaves

finely grated zest of 1 small lemon

1 tablespoon extra-virgin olive oil,
plus extra for drizzling

1.2 kg boneless pork belly,
skin scored at 1 cm intervals

DF, GF | **SERVES 6–8**

With crispy crackling and tender juicy pork stuffed with a fragrant mix of piney sage, brash fennel and lemon, this porchetta looks super impressive but is very easy to master. To achieve perfect skin that puffs and crackles every time, it's essential to first remove the enemy of crispiness: moisture. Leave your rolled porchetta uncovered in the fridge overnight so the skin gets rubbery and dry. Pop it in the oven the next day and you will be rewarded with the crunchiest crackling and most succulent pork.

Combine the fennel seeds, peppercorns and salt in a mortar and crush with the pestle. Add the garlic and sage and pound to combine. Mix in the lemon zest and olive oil to form a paste.

Rub the paste onto the meat side of the pork. Roll up to enclose the paste and tie with kitchen string at 2 cm intervals. Sprinkle a generous pinch of salt onto the skin and massage firmly into the crevices. Place the porchetta, seam-side down, on a wire rack in a roasting tin. Refrigerate, uncovered, overnight to dry out the skin.

The next day, remove the porchetta from the fridge an hour before cooking so it can come to room temperature.

Preheat the oven to 250°C (fan-forced).

Drizzle a little olive oil onto the skin and massage it in well. Roast for 20 minutes, then reduce the oven temperature to 140°C and roast for 1 hour or until the porchetta is golden and crispy. Rest for 20 minutes before carving.

NOTE

—Leftover porchetta makes the ultimate filling for crusty gluten-free rolls the next day. Simply fill the rolls with porchetta slices, a handful of rocket and some creamy lemon aioli or zesty salsa verde.

Afelia
Pork with Red Wine & Coriander Seeds

1 kg boneless pork shoulder, cut into 6 cm chunks

500 ml (2 cups) dry red wine

sea salt flakes and freshly ground black pepper

3 tablespoons extra-virgin olive oil

1 onion, finely chopped

2 tablespoons coriander seeds, lightly crushed

3 fresh bay leaves

3 garlic cloves, finely chopped

2 tablespoons tomato paste

cooked basmati rice, potatoes or quinoa, to serve

dollop of Greek yoghurt, to serve (optional)

coriander leaves, to serve

DFO, GF | SERVES 4–6

Afelia is a traditional Cypriot dish thrown together with just a handful of ingredients. This recipe was taught to me by my Cypriot neighbours when I was a young adult. I always associate the citrusy aroma of gently crushed coriander seeds with Cypriot food as they feature heavily in recipes from this beautiful island. This is a very low-effort dish that delivers maximum flavour – an easy wintery dinner.

Place the pork and wine in a large non-reactive bowl, cover and marinate overnight in the fridge (you can skip this step, but the flavour won't be as intense). The next day, remove the pork with a slotted spoon and transfer to a tray. Reserve the wine. Season the pork all over with salt and pepper.

Heat 2 tablespoons of the olive oil in a large heavy-based saucepan over medium–high heat. Sear the pork, in batches, for 10 minutes or until browned all over. Remove from the pan and set aside.

Reduce the heat to low and heat the remaining oil in the pan. Add the onion, coriander seeds and bay leaves and sauté for 2 minutes to soften the onion. Stir in the garlic and tomato paste and cook for another minute. Deglaze the pan with the reserved red wine, stirring to release any caramelised bits caught on the base.

Return the pork and resting juices to the pan, add 125 ml (½ cup) of water and bring to a simmer. Cover and cook, turning the pork occasionally, for 1½–2 hours or until the pork is tender. If the sauce looks too thin, simmer, uncovered, until it has a slightly syrupy consistency. Serve with your choice of rice, potatoes or quinoa and add a dollop of yoghurt, if desired. Scatter with coriander to finish.

Brizoles
Chargrilled Pork Chops

4 x 200 g bone-in pork chops, fat scored

Tzatziki (page 208) and lemon wedges, to serve (optional)

DIJON MARINADE

2 tablespoons extra-virgin olive oil

2 garlic cloves, crushed

1 teaspoon dijon mustard

3 teaspoons sea salt flakes

1 teaspoon dried oregano

¼ teaspoon freshly ground white pepper

GF, DFO | **SERVES 4**

Pork chops can get a bad rap for being dry or bland, often the result of overcooking and poor seasoning. These glistening garlicky chops are your express ticket to tender, juicy, flavoursome pork every time.

A few simple rules to remember. First, take your pork out of the fridge at least 30 minutes prior to grilling for an even cook. Second, render and sear the side fat on the chops for crispy, golden edges. Third, rest your meat for 5 minutes before serving so the pork juices don't run out. You will always get the crispiest, smokiest finish on a hot charcoal barbecue, but rest assured you can also achieve great results in a hot chargrill pan any night of the week.

Combine the dijon marinade ingredients in a bowl and whisk well.

Place the pork on a tray and massage the marinade all over the meat. Marinate for 30 minutes at room temperature or cover and transfer to the fridge to marinate overnight.

Heat a chargrill pan or barbecue grill plate over medium–high heat. Sear the chops sideways (fat-side down) for 4 minutes to render the fat. Once the fat is crispy, lay the chops flat in the pan and cook for 3–4 minutes on each side until golden and crisp. Serve with optional tzatziki and lemon wedges.

Soutzoukakia
Baked Meatballs in Red Sauce

cooked basmati rice or gluten-free pasta, to serve

MEATBALLS

2 teaspoons sea salt flakes

pinch of freshly ground black pepper

1 large all-purpose potato (such as sebago), peeled and finely grated, excess moisture squeezed out

250 g pork mince

250 g beef mince

1 onion, grated, excess moisture squeezed out

2 garlic cloves, finely grated

handful of flat-leaf parsley leaves, finely chopped, plus extra to serve

handful of mint leaves, finely chopped

1 teaspoon ground cumin

1 teaspoon ground cinnamon

½ teaspoon dried oregano

1 egg

RED SAUCE

80 ml (⅓ cup) extra-virgin olive oil

1 large onion, finely chopped

pinch of sea salt flakes

1 garlic clove, finely grated

125 ml (½ cup) red wine

2 x 400 g cans crushed tomatoes

½ teaspoon caster sugar

1 teaspoon dried oregano

2 fresh bay leaves

½ teaspoon allspice

pinch of grated nutmeg

3 whole cloves

My paternal grandparents were Greek refugees from Asia Minor (now mostly modern-day Turkey). I met them only once on my first trip to Greece when I was ten. At the time, I didn't understand why they spoke to each other in Turkish. Much later I discovered that for many years they were forbidden to speak Greek under Turkish rule. In 1922 at the end of the Greco–Turkish War, during a population exchange between the two countries, they were forced to abandon their home and settled in northern Greece, bringing many dishes from Asia Minor with them. Soutzoukakia was one of those recipes.

During my stay with my grandmother, she baked these mouthwatering cumin- and cinnamon-scented meatballs in rich tomato sauce for me. Now I make gluten-free soutzoukakia for my kids, and swap out the bread in the mince mixture with finely grated potato to keep the meatballs super light and fluffy. The intoxicating aroma of the simmering sauce still takes me straight back to Yiayia's village kitchen. I love that this warming and delicious recipe is imbued with the history of my father's family.

Combine the meatball ingredients in a large bowl and mix well with your hands. Cover and rest in the fridge for 30 minutes, then roll the mixture into 16 oval-shaped logs. Transfer to a baking dish.

For the red sauce, heat the olive oil in a large frying pan over medium heat, add the onion and salt and sauté, stirring occasionally, for 8 minutes to soften. Stir in the garlic and cook for 30 seconds. Deglaze the pan with the red wine, stirring to release any caramelised bits caught on the base, and simmer for 2–3 minutes or until reduced by half. Add the tomatoes, caster sugar, herbs and spices, stir to combine and simmer for 20 minutes to thicken the sauce.

Preheat the oven to 200°C (fan-forced).

Pour the sauce over meatballs and bake for 20 minutes until rich and golden. Serve with cooked rice or pasta and a sprinkling of parsley over the top.

DF, GF | SERVES 4–6

Beef Koftas with Pomegranate Tahini

extra-virgin olive oil, for brushing

squeeze of lemon juice

pomegranate seeds (optional)

KOFTAS

600 g beef mince

1 small red onion, grated, excess moisture squeezed out

2 garlic cloves, crushed

2 teaspoons ground cumin

1 teaspoon sumac

3 tablespoons finely chopped flat-leaf parsley leaves, plus extra leaves to serve

3 tablespoons finely chopped mint leaves, plus extra leaves to serve

3 teaspoons sea salt flakes

pinch of freshly ground black pepper

POMEGRANATE TAHINI

3 tablespoons tahini

2 tablespoons pomegranate molasses

1 tablespoon freshly squeezed lemon juice

pinch of sea salt flakes and freshly ground black pepper

DF, GF | SERVES 4–6

Every Mediterranean culture has its own version of meatballs: Spanish albondigas, Italian polpettes and Greek keftedes. Throw in the big intoxicating flavours of the Middle East and koftas come out as a clear winner with my kids, who love anything delicious on a stick. To cut through the richness of the spiced meat, here, I pair the koftas with a sweet and sour pomegranate tahini sauce – which can be slathered over them in a wrap or dolloped on the side. Serve with a vibrant shredded salad.

Combine the kofta ingredients in a bowl and mix with your hands. Cover the bowl and rest in the fridge for 30 minutes.

Soak ten flat bamboo skewers in water for 30 minutes.

With damp hands, mould the kofta mixture evenly onto the skewers in a long flat shape.

Place a chargrill pan over high heat. Brush the koftas with olive oil and cook, turning once, for 5 minutes or until charred and just cooked through. Squeeze over the lemon juice and set aside.

Whisk the pomegranate tahini ingredients in a bowl to form a paste. Add a little water to thin out to the desired consistency and whisk again. Serve with the koftas, extra herbs and pomegranate seeds (if using).

VARIATION

— The beef can be replaced with lamb mince and other Mediterranean spices can be used, such as allspice, ground coriander, cayenne pepper and ground cinnamon.

Koupes
Quinoa-crusted Beef Croquettes

sunflower oil, for shallow-frying

Greek yoghurt and lemon wedges, to serve

QUINOA DOUGH

250 g (1¼ cups) white quinoa, rinsed

sea salt flakes

½ teaspoon ground cinnamon

pinch of freshly ground white pepper

BEEF FILLING

1 tablespoon extra-virgin olive oil

1 onion, finely chopped

sea salt flakes and freshly ground black pepper

250 g beef mince

1 large garlic clove, finely chopped

2 tablespoons pine nuts

½ teaspoon ground cinnamon

½ teaspoon ground cumin

handful of flat-leaf parsley leaves, finely chopped, plus extra leaves to serve

handful of mint leaves, finely chopped, plus extra leaves to serve

½ teaspoon finely grated lemon zest

GF, VO | SERVES 6–8

Koupes are a Cypriot street food, similar to Middle Eastern kibbeh. Traditionally, koupes contain a fragrant beef mince filling encased in a cracked bulgur wheat crust. I have given them a gluten-free makeover and replaced the bulgur with quinoa – and the results are spectacular. The quinoa shell is so light and crispy you will not notice the swap. These are so delicious it's hard to stop at one.

To make the quinoa dough, place the quinoa in a saucepan, add 625 ml (2½ cups) of water, cover and simmer over low heat for 10 minutes. Remove from the heat and cool with the lid on, then fluff with a fork. Transfer the quinoa to a food processor and season with 1 teaspoon of salt, the cinnamon and white pepper. Blitz to form a coarse paste. Set aside to cool completely.

To make the beef filling, heat the olive oil in a large frying pan over medium–low heat. Add the onion and a pinch of salt and sauté, stirring occasionally, for 5 minutes or until softened. Add the beef and cook, breaking up large chunks with a wooden spoon, for 2–3 minutes until browned. Stir in the garlic, pine nuts, cinnamon, cumin and a good pinch of salt and black pepper. Cook for another minute to combine. Remove from the heat and stir in the parsley, mint and lemon zest. Taste and adjust the seasoning if necessary.

Roll the cooled quinoa dough into 16 balls. Press a ball between the palms of your hands to flatten into a thin disc. Place a heaped tablespoon of mince filling in the centre of the disc. Fold the disc over to seal the filling and, using your hands, shape into an oval. Repeat this process with the remaining quinoa balls and filling.

Heat enough sunflower oil for shallow-frying in a large, deep frying pan until it reaches 180°C on a kitchen thermometer (or until a cube of gluten-free bread dropped in the hot oil browns in 15 seconds). Add the koupes in batches and fry for 5–6 minutes or until golden and crunchy. Drain on paper towel. Serve with Greek yoghurt, lemon wedges and a sprinkling of extra herbs.

VARIATION

—Vegetarian Koupes: replace the mince with 250 g chopped mushrooms of your choice.

NUTRITION NOTE

—Quinoa is a complete protein containing all nine essential amino acids. It is a great source of fibre, antioxidants and minerals, so it is nutritionally superior to bulgur wheat and couscous.

Kleftiko
Lamb Parcels

1 kg boneless lamb shoulder
(you can ask a butcher to debone
it for you), excess fat trimmed,
cut into large chunks

2 tablespoons extra-virgin olive oil

4 garlic cloves, crushed

2 teaspoons dried oregano

sea salt flakes and freshly ground
black pepper

2 large waxy potatoes (such
as desiree or pontiac), cut
into wedges

3 tomatoes, each cut into 4 wedges

150 g kefalograviera cheese,
cut into 3 cm cubes

juice of 1 lemon

8 thyme sprigs

DFO, GF | SERVES 4

Kleftiko is a classic Greek lamb recipe steeped in a rich history.
The dish is named after the Klephtes, a group of bandits who fought
the Ottomans and slow-cooked lamb in underground pits to avoid
detection. There is no need to dig a pit here; just wrap chunks of
lamb shoulder in individual parcels to trap the steam and you will
have the most meltingly tender meat. The potatoes sitting under the
meat soak up the beautiful lamb juices and the cheese cubes melt into
delicious nuggets of stretchy goodness. The excitement and theatre
of unwrapping these parcels at the dinner table is matched by the
stunning flavour and aroma. This is the perfect dinner party recipe.

Preheat the oven to 160°C (fan-forced).

Place the lamb in a large shallow bowl and add the olive oil, garlic, oregano
and a good pinch of salt and pepper. Massage the seasoning all over the
lamb (you can marinate it overnight in the fridge if you wish).

Tear off eight 20 cm × 30 cm sheets of baking paper and lay four sheets on
your workbench. Place the remaining sheets on top in a crisscross manner
to create four double layers. Divide the potato wedges equally among the
parcels, then sit the lamb on top, so the juices fall on the wedges when
roasting. Divide the tomato and cheese equally among the parcels by
scattering them around the lamb. Drizzle the lemon juice on each bundle
and place two sprigs of thyme on the lamb. Wrap up each parcel by folding
the paper over the lamb and twisting the top to create a seal. Tightly secure
with kitchen string (it is very important that no steam escapes).

Place the four parcels on a baking tray and bake for 2 hours. To check for
tenderness, unwrap a parcel and pierce the lamb with a fork. The meat
should be very tender; if not, return to the oven for another 30 minutes.
Transfer the parcels to individual dinner plates to serve.

VARIATIONS
— For a dairy-free option, omit the cheese.
— You can swap the kefalograviera for Greek feta.

NOTE
— I like to prepare this dish with deboned lamb as it is easier to wrap
and eat, but you can use 1.6 kg bone-in lamb shoulder if you prefer.
If you are cooking lamb on the bone, ask your butcher to cut the
lamb shoulder into four portions, then bake the parcels for another
30 minutes until the lamb is meltingly tender.

Paidakia
Crispy Lamb Ribs

3 x 500 g lamb rib racks, fat trimmed

lemon wedges, to serve

SPICE MIX

1½ tablespoons sea salt flakes

1 tablespoon garlic powder

2 teaspoons dried oregano

2 teaspoons ground cumin

1 teaspoon sweet paprika

¼ teaspoon freshly ground black pepper

DF, GF | **SERVES 4–6**

I love all types of ribs – sticky, sweet, charred – but my favourite are those with a dry spice rub and a crispy crust. If you've never cooked ribs before, the good news is this simple method is virtually failproof. The Mediterranean spice mix comes together in seconds and all that follows is an easy two-step process. First, for tender meat, wrap the ribs tightly like a Christmas present so the hot trapped steam breaks down the collagen, then finish them off under a hot grill until crispy and charred.

Preheat the oven to 160°C (fan-forced).

Place a 30 cm × 60 cm sheet of foil on a large baking tray. Lay a sheet of baking paper of equal size on the foil, then place the ribs on top.

Combine the spice mix in a bowl, then firmly massage the mix all over the ribs. Cover the ribs with another sheet of baking paper. Using only both sheets of baking paper, tightly enclose the ribs to form a parcel. Repeat this process with the foil so you have a tightly wrapped parcel (you may need to use some extra foil sheets layered in the opposite direction to achieve this).

Bake for 2 hours or until the meat is tender. Remove the tray from the oven and turn the oven grill to high. Using kitchen scissors, carefully cut open the top of the parcel to uncover the ribs. Spoon the lamb juices in the parcel over the meat, then place the ribs under the hot grill for 5 minutes or until golden and crisp. Serve with lemon wedges.

TIPS

—To cut down on your preparation time and ensure your ribs are not overly fatty, ask your butcher to trim the fatty cap on the ribs.

—Placing a sheet of baking paper between the foil and the meat prevents the meat from sticking to the foil and creates an extra layer of insulation to trap the steam.

SYRUPY

SWE

Loukoumades
Honey–Walnut Doughnuts

195 g (1½ cups) gluten-free plain flour, sifted

40 g (⅓ cup) gluten-free cornflour, sifted

7 g sachet dried yeast

2 teaspoons caster sugar

pinch of sea salt flakes

sunflower oil, for deep-frying and greasing

honey, crushed walnuts and ground cinnamon, to serve

DF, GF, V, VGO | **MAKES 15**

What's the secret to golden gluten-free loukoumades with a crispy crust and fluffy centre? Cornflour! When combined with gluten-free plain flour, cornflour produces a beautiful crunch, preventing the dreaded culinary pitfall of soggy loukoumades. A bubbly, airy dough produces a lighter doughnut, so ensure you give your yeasted dough enough time to rise. Get this part right and I guarantee you fluffy balls of crisp perfection every time. All that's left is a drizzling of honey, a sprinkling of nuts and a dusting of cinnamon. It will be hard to stop at one.

Combine the flour, cornflour, yeast, sugar and salt in a bowl and mix with a wooden spoon. Pour in 375 ml (1½ cups) of lukewarm water and mix to form a soft, wet dough. Cover the bowl with plastic wrap and rest in a warm spot for 2 hours or until the dough has at least doubled in size and is bubbly and airy.

Heat enough sunflower oil for deep-frying in a large, deep frying pan until it reaches 180°C on a kitchen thermometer (or until a cube of gluten-free bread dropped in the oil browns in 15 seconds). Dip a tablespoon in some oil (the oil prevents the dough from sticking to the spoon), then scoop a walnut-sized ball of dough from the bowl and drop the dough directly into the hot oil. Repeat this process until your pan is filled with several balls but is not overcrowded.

Fry the doughnuts, turning occasionally with a slotted spoon for even browning, for 4–5 minutes or until golden and crisp. Remove with the slotted spoon and transfer to a platter. Immediately drizzle with a generous amount of honey, sprinkle on some crushed walnuts and dust with cinnamon. Serve warm. Loukoumades should be eaten on the day they are made.

VARIATIONS
—You could also try these topping ideas: sesame seeds, crushed pistachios, maple syrup, Nutella or caramel sauce.

Karithopita
Walnut Syrup Cake

200 g (2 cups) walnuts

375 ml (1½ cups) light olive oil

230 g (1 cup) caster sugar

4 eggs, at room temperature

2 tablespoons brandy

2 teaspoons vanilla extract

260 g (2 cups) gluten-free
self-raising flour, sifted

2 teaspoons ground cinnamon

handful of crushed walnuts
(mixed with ground cinnamon
if you like), to serve

SPICED SUGAR SYRUP

345 g (1½ cups) caster sugar

finely grated zest and juice of
1 small lemon

1 cinnamon stick

3 whole cloves

DF, GF, V | **SERVES 20**

Karithopita is a mouthwatering, fluffy cinnamon and walnut cake soaked in lemon syrup. Perfecting this cake is all about balance: I'm not a fan of overly sweet cakes and think it's important to get the ratio of sponge to syrup correct to avoid a sickly sweet or too heavily soaked cake. Some people make karithopita with butter, but I prefer to follow the ancient Greek tradition of using olive oil as the base for a beautifully moist and completely dairy-free cake.

To make the spiced sugar syrup, place the sugar, lemon zest and juice, cinnamon, cloves and 500 ml (2 cups) of water in a small saucepan. Stir to combine and bring to the boil, then reduce the heat to low and simmer for 8 minutes to reduce and thicken. Set aside to cool slightly, then transfer to a heatproof bowl and place in the fridge to cool completely.

Preheat the oven to 170°C (fan-forced). Brush a 30 cm round or 30 cm × 23 cm rectangular cake tin with light olive oil.

Blitz or pound the walnuts to a coarse meal. Set aside.

Place the olive oil, sugar, eggs, brandy and vanilla in the bowl of an electric mixer fitted with the paddle attachment and beat on medium speed to just bring the ingredients together. Add the flour and cinnamon and mix to combine. Add the walnut meal and mix on low speed until just combined. Pour the wet batter into the prepared tin, spreading it a little higher around the rim to allow for an even rise. Bake for 40 minutes or until golden and an inserted skewer comes out clean.

Slice the cake in the tin into squares or diamonds. Pour the cooled syrup over the hot cake, then decorate the centre of each piece with the crushed walnuts. Set aside for 2 hours so the cake soaks up the syrup, then serve. Store in an airtight container at room temperature for up to 5 days.

NOTES

— The golden rule when making a syrup cake is to pour cold syrup over a hot cake or hot syrup over a cold cake. This technique prevents your cake from turning soggy.

— It is important to use the correct tin size for an even distribution of syrup. If your cake is smaller and taller, you risk a syrupy base and dry top.

Kolokithopita
Pumpkin Pie with Walnut & Honey

1 x quantity Olive Oil Pastry
(page 206)

light olive oil, for brushing

½ teaspoon caster sugar mixed
with ¼ teaspoon ground cinnamon

115 g (⅓ cup) honey

PUMPKIN FILLING

300 g butternut pumpkin,
finely grated, excess moisture
squeezed out

100 g (1 cup) walnuts, coarsely
crushed, plus extra for sprinkling

80 g (⅓ cup) caster sugar

2 teaspoons ground cinnamon,
plus extra for dusting

¼ teaspoon ground cloves

DF, GF, V | **SERVES 8–10**

Of all the coiled pastry recipes my mother has taught me, this is probably my favourite. There are many different versions of Greek pumpkin pie ('kolokithi' meaning pumpkin and 'pita' meaning pie), some sweet some savoury. I'm obsessed with the sweet version because it tastes just like baklava with the added bonus of soft cinnamon-spiked pumpkin in the filling. The contrasting textures and flavours are just spectacular. My olive oil pastry works perfectly here as a gluten-free and dairy-free alternative to traditional filo.

Preheat the oven to 200°C (fan-forced) and grease a 24 cm round cake tin with olive oil.

Combine the pumpkin filling ingredients in a bowl and mix well.

Divide the cold pastry into four portions. Working with one portion at a time, place the pastry between two large sheets of baking paper. Roll out the pastry to the shape of a paper-thin rectangle roughly 50 cm × 10 cm. Remove the top layer of baking paper and place one quarter of the pumpkin filling in a log shape along the long edge of the pastry closest to you. Using the bottom sheet of baking paper to help, lift the dough and roll it over the filling to enclose and seal (only allow a 2 cm pastry overlap at the seam to keep the pastry fairly thin). Sit the log along the outer edge of the tin to create the outer coil. Repeat this process with the remaining dough and filling to create an inward spiral.

Brush the top of the coil with olive oil and sprinkle on the cinnamon sugar. Bake for 25 minutes or until the pastry is golden and crisp. Remove from the oven and immediately drizzle the honey over the top. Sprinkle on the extra walnuts and add a dusting of cinnamon. Set aside for 30 minutes so the pastry can soak up the syrup, then slice and serve. Store in an airtight container at room temperature for up to 3 days.

VARIATION
—You might like to add raisins or currants to your filling.

Baklava Fingers

1 x quantity Olive Oil Pastry
(page 206)

light olive oil, for brushing

115 g (⅓ cup) honey

BAKLAVA FILLING

50 g (½ cup) walnuts

40 g (¼ cup) almonds

1 teaspoon ground cinnamon,
plus extra for dusting (optional)

1 teaspoon caster sugar

DF, GF, V | **MAKES 12**

When I eliminated gluten from my diet, the dessert I missed most was baklava. It was virtually impossible to find gluten-free baklava, let alone gluten-free filo to recreate those wafer-thin pastry layers. This led me to experiment at home with my versatile olive oil pastry to create a baklava finger inspired by Cypriot 'dactyla' – or lady fingers – those deliciously crisp fried pastries stuffed with crushed nuts and drizzled with honey. I got to rolling and baking and they turned out perfectly – no messy fryer or layering necessary. These thin and crispy pastry fingers are stuffed with cinnamon-spiked walnuts and almonds and are drizzled with honey to finish. Everything you absolutely love about baklava in a crispy bite-sized finger.

Preheat the oven to 200°C (fan-forced) and line a baking tray with baking paper.

To make the baklava filling, crush the nuts to a coarse meal using either a mortar and pestle or food processor. Add the cinnamon and sugar and stir to combine.

Divide the pastry into three balls so it is easier to manage. Roll one ball between two sheets of baking paper until the pastry is paper thin. Slice the pastry into four 12 cm squares and brush the edges with olive oil. Place 2 teaspoons of the nut filling in a strip along one edge of each square. Roll the pastry over the filling into a cigar and seal each end by gently pressing down with a fork. Transfer the baklava fingers to the prepared tray and brush with oil. Repeat with the remaining dough and filling, saving some of the filling to sprinkle over the cooked baklava.

Bake the baklava fingers for 15 minutes or until the pastry is golden. Remove the tray from the oven and immediately drizzle the honey over the top. Sprinkle on the remaining nut filling and dust with extra cinnamon, if desired. Store in an airtight container at room temperature for up to 3 days.

Coconut Syrup Cake

150 g unsalted butter, softened

230 g (1 cup) caster sugar

3 eggs, at room temperature

125 ml (½ cup) milk

1 teaspoon finely grated lemon zest

1 tablespoon cognac (optional)

180 g (2 cups) desiccated coconut, plus 45 g (½ cup) extra for sprinkling

260 g (2 cups) self-raising gluten-free flour, sifted

1 tablespoon gluten-free baking powder

SUGAR SYRUP

345 g (1½ cups) caster sugar

finely grated zest and juice of 1 lemon

GF, V | SERVES 12–14

Of all the syrupy sponge cakes, this is probably the easiest to bake and most universally loved because it is so light, airy and refreshing. The fluffy coconut sponge soaks up all the lemon syrup, producing an utterly delicious, moist cake. Start by preparing your syrup so it has plenty of time to cool before pouring over your hot cake. Remember: cold syrup over hot cake or hot syrup over cold cake.

This cake tastes even better the next day; feel free to bake ahead so the sponge has plenty of time to soak up the gorgeous zesty syrup.

To make the sugar syrup, combine the sugar and lemon zest and juice in a small saucepan, add 500 ml (2 cups) of water, stir and bring to the boil. Reduce the heat to low and simmer for 8 minutes to thicken. Carefully pour the hot syrup into a heatproof bowl and set aside in the fridge to cool completely while you prepare the cake.

Preheat the oven to 160°C (fan-forced) and generously grease a 23 cm bundt tin with butter.

Place the butter and sugar in the bowl of an electric mixer fitted with the paddle attachment and beat for 5 minutes on medium speed or until light and fluffy. With the mixer on low speed, beat in the eggs, one at a time, until fully incorporated. Add the milk, lemon zest, cognac (if using) and coconut and beat until combined. Next, add the flour and baking powder and beat until just combined. Spoon the batter into the prepared tin, smooth the top and bake for 40 minutes or until an inserted skewer comes out clean.

While the cake is still hot and in its tin, use a toothpick to pierce about 10 deep holes all over the sponge so the syrup soaks up evenly. Slowly pour the cooled syrup over the hot cake. Rest for a couple of minutes so the cake soaks up the syrup, then transfer to a platter or cake stand and sprinkle on the extra coconut. Set aside for at least 1 hour, then serve. Store in an airtight container at room temperature for up to 5 days.

Revani
Polenta Syrup Cake

125 g unsalted butter, softened

230 g (1 cup) caster sugar

3 eggs, at room temperature, separated

250 g (1 cup) Greek yoghurt

1 teaspoon vanilla extract

1 teaspoon finely grated lemon zest

150 g (1 cup) polenta

130 g (1 cup) gluten-free self-raising flour

2 teaspoons gluten-free baking powder

½ teaspoon bicarbonate of soda

20 blanched almonds

LEMON SYRUP

345 g (1½ cups) caster sugar

juice of 1 small lemon

5 cm strip of lemon rind

2 teaspoons orange blossom water (optional)

GF, V | **SERVES 20**

Syrup-soaked semolina cakes are prevalent throughout the Mediterranean and can be found in most countries of the former Ottoman Empire – basbousa in Egypt, namoura in Lebanon and revani in Turkey, Albania and Greece. They are all slightly different versions of what is essentially the same cake – syrup-soaked semolina sponge baked and sliced into diamonds or squares. To give this ancient classic a gluten-free makeover, I replace the semolina with polenta for that same grittiness to soak up the syrup – and it works perfectly. What results is an incredibly moist, light and fluffy sponge with slightly chewy, crunchy edge pieces (always the best parts).

To make the lemon syrup, combine the sugar, lemon juice, lemon rind and 375 ml (1½ cups) of water in a small saucepan over high heat. Bring to the boil, stirring occasionally, then reduce the heat to low and simmer for 5 minutes to thicken. Remove the pan from the heat and stir in the orange blossom water (if using). Carefully pour the hot syrup into a heatproof bowl and set aside in the fridge to cool completely while you prepare the cake.

Preheat the oven to 160°C (fan-forced) and grease a 28 cm round or square cake tin with butter.

Place the butter and sugar in the bowl of an electric mixer fitted with the paddle attachment and beat on medium speed for 5 minutes or until light and fluffy. With the mixer on low speed, beat in the egg yolks, one at a time, until fully incorporated. Add the yoghurt, vanilla and lemon zest and beat well, then beat in the polenta, flour, baking powder and bicarbonate of soda until just combined.

In a separate bowl, whisk the egg whites until soft peaks form. Gently fold the egg whites into the batter, one-third at a time, until just combined. Pour the batter into the prepared tin, then use a knife to score diamonds or squares into the batter. Sit one blanched almond in the centre of each shape. Bake for 40–45 minutes or until golden and an inserted skewer comes out clean.

Slice the cake along the scored lines to allow the syrup to soak in. Pour the cooled syrup over the hot cake. Set aside for 1 hour so the sponge soaks up the syrup, then serve. Store in an airtight container at room temperature for up to 5 days.

CAKES
&

BISCUITS

Vasilopita
New Year's Day Cake

400 g unsalted butter, softened (see Notes)

310 g (1⅓ cups) caster sugar

4 eggs, at room temperature

125 ml (½ cup) milk

2 tablespoons brandy

1 tablespoon vanilla extract

2 teaspoons mahlepi (see Notes)

½ teaspoon mastiha (see Notes)

finely grated zest and juice of 1 orange

500 g gluten-free self-raising flour, sifted

½ teaspoon bicarbonate of soda

pure icing sugar, sifted, for dusting

GF, V | SERVES 12

Depending on the region of Greece there are two quite different versions of Vasilopita: the cake (this recipe) or the tsoureki brioche (which is the same as Easter tsoureki; page 28). Vasilopita is sliced on New Year's Day to bless the house and bring good luck for the new year. Each family member receives a slice and whoever discovers the coin hidden inside the cake is said to be granted luck for that year.

For the best result, it is very important to beat the butter and sugar well until fluffy and creamy. Get this step right and you will be rewarded with a light and airy sponge, featuring spectacular notes of orange, musky mastiha and fruity mahlepi; a distinctive flavour combination you will not find anywhere else.

Preheat the oven to 160°C (fan-forced). Grease and line a 30 cm round cake tin with baking paper.

Place the butter and caster sugar in the bowl of an electric mixer fitted with the paddle attachment and beat on medium speed, scraping down the side of the bowl once or twice, for 5 minutes or until light and fluffy. With the mixer on low speed, beat in the eggs, one at a time, until just incorporated. Add the milk, brandy, vanilla, mahlepi and mastiha and beat until combined. Beat in the orange zest and juice, then mix in the flour and bicarbonate of soda until just combined.

Transfer the batter to the prepared tin (at this point you have the option of wrapping a coin in foil and hiding it in the batter). Bake for 40 minutes or until an inserted skewer comes out clean. Cool the cake in the tin, then turn out onto a platter. Dust the cake with icing sugar and serve. Store in an airtight container at room temperature for up to 3 days.

NOTES

— For a light and fluffy cake, it is essential to start with well softened butter. Your butter should be soft enough for your finger to make an imprint with no resistance.

— Mahlepi and mastiha can both be found at European delis and gourmet grocers.

— Create decorative patterns by placing cookie cutters or paper stencils on top of the cake prior to dusting with icing sugar.

Fanouropita
Spiced Vegan Cake

1 teaspoon finely grated
orange zest

310 ml (1¼ cups) freshly squeezed
orange juice

1 teaspoon bicarbonate of soda

185 ml (¾ cup) light olive oil

230 g (1 cup) caster sugar

2 tablespoons brandy (optional)

260 g (2 cups) gluten-free
self-raising flour, sifted

1 teaspoon ground cinnamon

¼ teaspoon ground cloves

90 g (¾ cup) roughly chopped
walnuts or almonds

60 g (½ cup) raisins

pure icing sugar, sifted, for dusting

DF, GF, VG | SERVES 10

Fanouropita is an aromatic vegan cake baked on 27 August, in honour of the Greek Saint Fanourios (the saint of 'lost things'), and eaten during religious periods of fasting. This cake has an old tradition, dating back to 1500 AD, when worshippers would ask Saint Fanourios to help find lost people or objects. In exchange, they thanked him with this cake. Requiring only a few pantry staples, this deliciously moist cinnamon- and clove-scented sponge is studded with sweet juicy raisins and chopped nuts for beautiful texture and flavour.

This is an easy tea cake a first-time baker can master in minutes.

Preheat the oven to 170°C (fan-forced) and grease a 20 cm square cake tin.

Place the orange zest and juice and bicarbonate of soda in a bowl and whisk until frothy. Add the olive oil, caster sugar and brandy (if using) and whisk to combine. Add the flour, cinnamon and cloves and mix with a wooden spoon to incorporate. Fold in the nuts and raisins.

Spoon the batter into the prepared tin and bake for 35–40 minutes or until an inserted skewer comes out clean. Cool the cake in the tin, then turn out onto a platter. Dust the cake with icing sugar and serve. Store in an airtight container at room temperature for up to 5 days.

Fluffy Lemon, Ricotta & Blueberry Loaf

160 g unsalted butter, softened

345 g (1½ cups) caster sugar

400 g fresh ricotta, drained

3 eggs, at room temperature

2 teaspoons vanilla extract

finely grated zest and juice of
1 small lemon

195 g (1½ cups) gluten-free
self-raising flour, sifted

125 g blueberries, plus extra
to serve (optional)

finely sliced lemon peel,
to serve (optional)

LEMON GLAZE (OPTIONAL)

155 g (1¼ cups) pure icing
sugar, sifted

1 teaspoon freshly squeezed
lemon juice

1 egg white

GF, V | **SERVES 10**

What I love most about Italian baked cakes is their simplicity. They are not overly sweet or adorned; rather, they rely on a few pantry staples that any home baker can throw together. Take your time with the first step in this recipe and you will be rewarded with the lightest, fluffiest ricotta cake that is bursting with citrus flavour. It is critical to beat your butter, sugar and ricotta very well for a super light and airy batter.

I have studded my cake with blueberries for juicy bursts of fruit, but feel free to omit this step for a classic plain ricotta loaf, just like the one sitting on every nonna's kitchen bench.

Preheat the oven to 160°C (fan-forced) and grease a 25 cm × 13 cm loaf tin with butter.

Place the butter and caster sugar in the bowl of an electric mixer fitted with the paddle attachment and beat on medium speed for 5 minutes or until light and fluffy. Scrape down the side of the bowl, add the ricotta and beat for 5 minutes to create an airy batter. Beat in the eggs, one at a time, until fully incorporated. Add the vanilla, lemon zest and juice and beat until combined, then mix in the flour until just incorporated. Fold in two-thirds of the blueberries.

Pour the batter into the prepared tin and scatter on the remaining berries. Bake for 50–60 minutes or until an inserted skewer comes out clean. Cool in the tin, then turn out onto a platter.

To make the lemon glaze (if using), whisk together the icing sugar, lemon juice and egg white. Immediately pour over the cooled cake, then garnish with lemon peel and extra blueberries, if desired. Store in an airtight container at room temperature for up to 3 days.

Mosaiko
No-bake Chocolate & Biscuit Log Cake

3 x 125 g packets gluten-free
Marie tea biscuits

170 ml (⅔ cup) warm milk

2 tablespoons cognac or brandy

200 g unsalted butter, softened

100 g pure icing sugar, sifted

200 g gluten-free dark chocolate
(70% cocoa), melted and cooled
slightly

dutch-process cocoa powder,
sifted, for dusting (optional)

GF, V | SERVES 10

Named after the mosaic pattern that is revealed once it is sliced, this is the easy no-bake dessert every kid in the street requested when they popped over for a visit. The combination of whipped butter and melted chocolate delivers a super silky texture. I'm not a fan of dry mosaics, so I soak my biscuits well in lukewarm milk to keep them moist before adding them to the buttercream. For added texture, feel free to include nuts or dried fruit. I have kept this recipe very simple – the way my kids love it – chocolate and biscuits, that's it! Don't forget the addition of cognac or brandy for mild liquor notes in the background.

Use your hands to break the biscuits into large chunks and place in a shallow bowl. Combine the milk and cognac or brandy in a bowl and drizzle the mixture over the biscuits. Gently toss and set aside for 10 minutes, tossing occasionally, until the biscuits soak up the milk mixture.

Place the butter and icing sugar in the bowl of an electric mixer fitted with the paddle attachment and beat on medium speed for 5 minutes or until light and fluffy. With the mixer on low speed, pour in the melted chocolate and beat until incorporated.

Line a 20 cm × 10 cm loaf tin with plastic wrap, allowing some overhang.

Add the moist biscuits to the chocolate mixture and gently fold to combine (at this point your mixture will look messy, but rest assured you will have a beautiful mosaic once sliced). Spoon the mixture into the prepared tin, gently pressing and smoothing with your spoon to remove any air bubbles. Fold over the plastic overhang to cover the mosaic. Firmly smooth the top with your hands to close any air gaps. Refrigerate for 4 hours or overnight to set.

Turn the cake out onto a platter, dust with the cocoa powder (if using) and slice to serve. Store any remaining cake in an airtight container in the fridge for up to a week.

VARIATIONS

— For a nutty mosaic, add 60 g (½ cup) of your favourite chopped nuts and reduce the biscuits by 50 g.

— For an alcohol-free version, simply omit the cognac or brandy.

NOTE

— This recipe works best using a thin gluten-free tea biscuit to soak up the warm milk and soften.

Pasta Flora
Apricot Jam Tart

50 g unsalted butter, softened

115 g (½ cup) caster sugar

1 large egg

2 teaspoons vanilla extract

200 g gluten-free plain flour

60 g almond meal

1 teaspoon gluten-free
baking powder

pinch of sea salt flakes

250 g apricot jam, plus extra
warmed jam for brushing

dollop of double cream,
to serve (optional)

GF, V | SERVES 8

Pasta flora is a buttery shortcrust jam tart enjoyed throughout the Mediterranean. The Greek version is most commonly made with apricot jam, but you can also use other jams like berry, cherry, quince or fig. The correct ratio of jam to pastry is important to ensure your tart is not overly sweet or too dry. When you spread the jam filling in the tart case it will appear quite thin but it is just the right amount of sweetness. You can use either a good-quality store-bought jam or make your own from scratch.

Place the butter and sugar in the bowl of an electric mixer fitted with the paddle attachment and beat on medium speed for 3 minutes or until light and fluffy. Beat in the egg and vanilla until combined. Add the flour, almond meal, baking powder and salt and mix until a soft dough forms. Knead the dough into a disc and wrap in plastic wrap. Rest in the fridge for 1 hour.

Preheat the oven to 160°C (fan-forced) and generously grease a shallow 23 cm tart tin with butter.

Divide the dough into two portions. Place one portion between two sheets of baking paper and roll out to form a 2 mm thick round. Using your baking paper, flip the dough into your tart tin and peel away the paper. Press the dough into the base and side of the tin to remove any air bubbles.

Spoon the jam onto the pastry and spread out to cover the base. Roll out the remaining dough between the sheets of baking paper until roughly 2 mm thick, then cut into 1 cm wide strips. Lay the strips in a lattice pattern over the jam. Bake the tart for 25 minutes or until golden. Brush the lattice with the extra warmed jam for a glossy finish. Cool slightly so the jam can set, then slice and serve with the cream, if desired. Store in an airtight container at room temperature for up to 3 days.

HOMEMADE APRICOT JAM

—Combine 500 g sliced apricots, 3 tablespoons of water and 2 tablespoons of freshly squeezed lemon juice in a saucepan and bring to the boil. Reduce the heat, cover and simmer for 15 minutes. Add 500 g caster sugar, stirring until the sugar dissolves. Simmer, uncovered, for 20 minutes until thickened. Blitz the jam to a puree and spoon into sterilised jars. Store your jam in a cool, dark spot for up to a year. Once opened, store in the fridge for up to a month.

Sokolatopita
Olive Oil Chocolate Cake with Olive Oil Icing

90 g (¾ cup) dutch-process
cocoa powder, sifted

½ teaspoon bicarbonate of soda

pinch of sea salt flakes

250 ml (1 cup) light olive oil

125 ml (½ cup) boiling water

370 g (2 cups lightly packed)
brown sugar

3 eggs, at room temperature

1 tablespoon vanilla extract

170 g (1⅓ cups) gluten-free
plain flour, sifted

fresh berries, to serve (optional)

OLIVE OIL ICING

125 g (1 cup) gluten-free icing
sugar mixture, sifted

40 g (⅓ cup) dutch-process
cocoa powder, sifted

125–170 ml (½–⅔ cup) light olive oil

DF, GF, V | **SERVES 12**

Many people who don't eat gluten also avoid or limit dairy, so I often get requests for cakes that are free of both. Olive oil is always my first choice for dairy-free baking. It keeps cakes incredibly moist and has all the added health benefits minus the nasty additives found in commercial dairy-free butter substitutes. In baking, light olive oil works best as the delicate flavour will not overpower your baked goods.

Chocolate and olive oil are a match made in heaven. The fruity notes of the oil pair beautifully with the bitterness of cocoa. If you've never made a chocolate olive oil icing, you'll be surprised at how quickly it comes together and how amazingly luscious it tastes. This is not a dense, heavy cake. Expect a light, fluffy, airy sponge everyone will love.

Preheat the oven to 160°C (fan-forced) and line a 25 cm × 30 cm baking tin with baking paper.

Whisk together the cocoa powder, bicarbonate of soda and salt in a large bowl. Pour in the olive oil and boiling water and whisk to incorporate. Add the brown sugar, eggs and vanilla and whisk until smooth. Finally, whisk in the flour until combined.

Pour the batter into the prepared tin and bake for 30 minutes or until an inserted skewer comes out clean. Cool in the tin, then turn out onto a platter.

To make the olive oil icing, combine the dry ingredients in a bowl. Slowly drizzle in the olive oil while continuously whisking until you achieve a thick spreadable consistency.

Spread the icing over the cooled cake and scatter with the berries (if using). Store in an airtight container at room temperature for up to 3 days.

Chocolate Roulade with Espresso Cream

6 eggs, separated, at room temperature

150 g caster sugar

150 g gluten-free dark chocolate (70% cocoa), melted and cooled slightly

dutch-process cocoa powder, sifted, for dusting

ESPRESSO CREAM

300 ml thickened cream

30 g (¼ cup) pure icing sugar, sifted

2 tablespoons cooled espresso coffee (or use 1 tablespoon boiling water combined with 2 teaspoons instant coffee)

GF, V | **SERVES 10**

Roulade originates from the French word 'rouler', which means 'to roll'. Classic roulade is naturally gluten free because it is flourless, relying only on eggs, sugar and chocolate to produce a feathery sponge. This cake is so light and airy that your fork literally glides through the sponge, taking the mouthwatering espresso cream with it. The combination of coffee and chocolate tastes like a cross between tiramisu and mocha. You can even add a shot of your favourite liquor to the cream for an adults-only version.

Preheat the oven to 160°C (fan-forced) and line a 25 cm × 35 cm swiss roll tin with baking paper.

Combine the egg yolks and sugar in the bowl of an electric mixer fitted with the paddle attachment and beat on medium speed for 3 minutes or until pale and frothy. Pour in the chocolate and mix to combine.

Whisk the egg whites in a separate bowl until soft peaks form. Gently fold the egg whites into the chocolate mixture, one-third at a time, until just incorporated. Spread the batter evenly in the prepared tin and bake for 13 minutes or until springy to touch in the centre. Set aside to cool for 5 minutes.

Place a sheet of baking paper on top of the swiss roll, then cover with a chopping board and flip the warm sponge onto the board. Peel away the top layer of baking paper, cover the sponge in a clean tea towel and set aside to cool completely.

In a clean bowl, whisk the espresso cream ingredients together until soft peaks form.

Remove the plastic wrap from the sponge and spread the espresso cream evenly over the cake, leaving a 1 cm border. Using the bottom layer of baking paper to help, lift the sponge from one of the short sides and gently roll up. Wrap the roulade in a clean tea towel and rest, seam-side down, in the fridge for 1 hour to set. Dust with the cocoa powder and slice to serve. Store in an airtight container in the fridge up to 3 days.

FILLING VARIATIONS

—Raspberry Jam Roulade: spread 2–3 tablespoons of raspberry jam over the sponge and cover in whipped cream (no need to add sugar).

—Nutella Hazelnut Roulade: mix 70 g (¼ cup) Nutella into the cream and spread over the sponge, then sprinkle 30 g (¼ cup) chopped toasted hazelnuts over the cream.

Ladokoulouria
Vegan Olive Oil Biscuits

125 ml (½ cup) light olive oil

155 g (1¼ cups) pure icing sugar, sifted

2 tablespoons port

1 teaspoon finely grated orange zest

80 ml (⅓ cup) freshly squeezed orange juice

325 g (2½ cups) gluten-free self-raising flour, sifted

1 teaspoon ground cinnamon

½ teaspoon ground cloves

40 g (¼ cup) sesame seeds

DF, GF, VG | **MAKES 20**

Ladokoulouria derive their name from 'ladi', the Greek word for oil. These fragrant olive oil biscuits are enjoyed with a strong black coffee during religious fasting periods when dairy and eggs are not permitted. Most Greek households have a stash stored in the pantry all-year round because they are so easy to prepare. All that's required is a bowl and whisk – though of course you can use an electric mixer for ease. The aromatic combination of warm cinnamon, cloves, citrus and port in a crispy sesame-coated biscuit is delicious. These vegan treats are not overly sweet and can be enjoyed any time of the day.

Place the olive oil, icing sugar, port, orange zest and juice in the bowl of an electric mixer fitted with the whisk attachment. Whisk on medium–high speed for 1 minute to dissolve the sugar. Add the flour, cinnamon and cloves and mix until a soft dough forms. Pop in the fridge for 30 minutes so the dough can firm up for rolling.

Preheat the oven to 180°C (fan-forced). Line a large baking tray with baking paper.

Place the sesame seeds in a shallow bowl. Roll the dough into 20 balls, then roll the dough balls in the sesame seeds to coat. Place the balls on the prepared tray and press down gently to flatten slightly. Using your finger, push down in the centre of each biscuit to create a hole, then rotate it in a circular motion to increase the hole to 3 cm wide (this helps form a neat ring). Bake for 20 minutes or until the biscuits are golden and crispy. Transfer to a wire rack to cool. Store in an airtight container at room temperature for up to 1 week.

VARIATIONS

— The port can be replaced with brandy or cognac.

— For an alcohol-free version, just omit the alcohol or use 1 tablespoon vanilla extract instead.

Pistachio Biscotti

50 g unsalted butter, softened

145 g (⅔ cup) caster sugar

2 teaspoons vanilla extract

2 teaspoons finely grated lemon or orange zest

3 eggs, at room temperature

260 g (2 cups) gluten-free plain flour, sifted

1½ teaspoons gluten-free baking powder

pinch of sea salt flakes

100 g (¾ cup) shelled pistachios

GF, V | MAKES 25

Crispy, crunchy, nutty and absolutely perfect for coffee dunking, no wonder this twice-baked classic is Italy's most-loved biscuit. A simple nut inclusion without too many distractions is my favourite, allowing the flavour of the nut to shine. Here, I've paired pistachios with vanilla and citrus – feel free to use either lemon or orange zest. The thickness and length of your biscotti depends on personal preference. I like my biscotti longer and thinner, so they are extra crunchy and easier to dunk in coffee.

Place the butter, sugar, vanilla and citrus zest in the bowl of an electric mixer fitted with the paddle attachment and beat on medium speed for 5 minutes or until light and fluffy. With the mixer on low speed, beat in the eggs, one at a time and scraping down the side of the bowl, until just incorporated. Add the flour, baking powder and salt and mix to form a thick dough. Fold in the pistachios, then cover the bowl and transfer the dough to the fridge to rest for 30 minutes.

Preheat the oven to 170°C (fan-forced) and line a baking tray with baking paper.

Transfer the rested dough to a workbench lined with a sheet of baking paper. Shape the dough into two 20 cm × 10 cm rectangular logs. Transfer the logs to the prepared tray and bake for 20 minutes or until slightly golden. Remove the tray from the oven and set aside to cool for 10 minutes.

Slice the logs into 1.5 cm thick fingers. Arrange the slices on the baking tray and return to the oven for 15–20 minutes (depending on how crunchy you like your biscotti) until the biscotti are golden. Transfer to a wire rack to cool. Store in an airtight container for up to 2 weeks.

VARIATIONS

— Pistachio & White Chocolate Biscotti: melt 50 g white chocolate and drizzle over each biscuit.

— Almond & Orange Biscotti: replace the pistachios with whole almonds and use orange zest.

— Chocolate & Sour Cherry Biscotti: omit the pistachios and citrus zest and replace with 75 g (½ cup) roughly chopped gluten-free dark chocolate (70% cocoa) and 65 g (⅓ cup) roughly chopped sour cherries.

Biskota Marmalades
Jam Biscuits

50 g unsalted butter, softened

115 g (½ cup) caster sugar

1 egg, at room temperature

2 teaspoons vanilla extract

½ teaspoon finely grated lemon zest

200 g gluten-free plain flour

60 g almond meal

1 teaspoon gluten-free baking powder

pinch of sea salt flakes

160 g (½ cup) raspberry jam

pure icing sugar, sifted, for dusting

GF, V | MAKES 24

I first fell in love with these biscuits because of their pretty shape and was intrigued by the way my mother treated her dough like a pizza – rolling it into a circle, slicing it into 8 triangles, then rolling each slice inwards to form a scroll. The technique sounds impressive but, trust me, it is very easy to execute. The addition of almond meal gives the dough extra buttery notes and prevents it from cracking when rolled. The lemon zest pairs beautifully with the raspberry jam filling.

Place the butter and caster sugar in the bowl of an electric mixer fitted with the paddle attachment and beat on medium speed for 3 minutes or until light and fluffy. Add the egg, vanilla and lemon zest and beat until incorporated. Add the flour, almond meal, baking powder and salt and mix until a soft dough forms. Knead the dough into a disc and cover with plastic wrap. Rest in the fridge for 1 hour.

Preheat the oven to 160°C (fan-forced) and line a baking tray with baking paper.

Separate the dough into three balls. Working with one ball at a time, place the dough between two sheets of baking paper and roll out to form a round slightly larger than a 23 cm dinner plate. Place the plate on the dough and trim around the edge with a sharp knife. Slice the round into eight pieces like a pizza. Place ½–1 teaspoon of jam on each slice closer to the outer edge. Gently roll each slice inwards to form a scroll. Transfer the scrolls to the prepared tray. Repeat the process with the remaining dough and jam.

Bake the scrolls for 15 minutes or until crispy. Transfer to a wire rack to cool. Dust with a little icing sugar to finish. Store in an airtight container for up to 2 weeks.

VARIATION

—For a chocolatey version, you can replace the jam with Nutella.

Twisted Koulouria
Chocolate & Vanilla Easter Biscuits

125 g unsalted butter, softened

230 g (1 cup) caster sugar

3 eggs, at room temperature

1 tablespoon vanilla extract

1 teaspoon finely grated lemon zest

1 teaspoon finely grated orange zest

2 teaspoons brandy or ouzo (optional)

455 g (3½ cups) gluten-free plain flour, sifted

3 teaspoons gluten-free baking powder

50 g gluten-free dark chocolate (70% cocoa), melted

light olive oil, for greasing

whisked egg, for brushing

GF, V | **MAKES 25–30**

Koulouria, the traditional Greek Easter biscuits, can be traced back to 3000 BC and the Minoan civilisation of Crete, and their popularity has never wavered. In this fun twist, the addition of chocolate to these simple vanilla butter biscuits not only looks striking, but also adds an element of surprise. If you prefer to keep your koulouria vanilla, omit the chocolate paste. Either way, don't wait for Easter; these are a delicious treat the whole family will love all year round.

Place the butter and sugar in the bowl of an electric mixer fitted with the paddle attachment and beat on medium speed for 5 minutes or until light and fluffy. With the mixer on low speed, beat in the eggs, one at a time, until fully incorporated. Add the vanilla, lemon and orange zests and brandy or ouzo (if using) and beat to combine. Add the flour and baking powder and beat to form a very soft dough.

Transfer half the dough to another bowl. Add the melted chocolate to the remaining dough and beat to form a chocolate dough.

Cover both bowls with plastic wrap and rest in the fridge for 1 hour to firm up the dough and make it easier to roll.

Preheat the oven to 160°C (fan-forced) and line two baking trays with baking paper.

Grease your hands with a little light olive oil to make the dough easier to roll. Working in batches so the dough remains chilled, take one-third of each dough colour out of the fridge. Take a tablespoon of each dough colour and roll into two thin logs roughly 15 cm long. Connect the top of the two logs and twist to form a braid. Place the koulouria on the prepared trays and brush with the whisked egg. Repeat with the remaining dough. Bake for 20 minutes or until golden. Transfer to a wire rack to cool. Store the koulouria in an airtight container for up to 2 weeks.

VARIATION
—For a mocha note, mix 1 teaspoon instant coffee with 1 teaspoon boiling water and add to the dough with the melted chocolate.

NOTES
—These koulouria bake crispy. If you prefer a softer, cake-like texture to your biscuits, add 3 tablespoons of milk to your dough.

—The dough can be made ahead, wrapped tightly in plastic wrap and frozen for up to 1 month. Thaw the frozen dough to room temperature before rolling out.

BASICS

Olive Oil Pastry

260 g (2 cups) gluten-free plain flour

½ teaspoon gluten-free baking powder

pinch of sea salt flakes

2 large eggs (see Note)

125 ml (½ cup) light olive oil

DF, GF, V | MAKES 16 INDIVIDUAL PIES OR 1 LARGE 30 CM PIE

Place the flour, baking powder and salt in a large bowl and mix well.

Whisk the eggs and olive oil together in another bowl.

Add the egg mixture and 3 tablespoons of warm water to the dry ingredients and mix to combine. Use your hands to knead the dough for a minute to form a smooth ball. Cover the bowl and rest the dough in the fridge for 1 hour before using.

NOTE

—Using eggs of a different size may result in a dough that is too wet or too dry (add more flour or water respectively). Look for 600 g egg cartons labelled 'large' with an average egg weight of 55 g.

STOCKS

Chicken Stock

1 kg chicken bones

1 large carrot, cut into thirds

1 large onion, halved

1 large celery stalk, cut into thirds

2 fresh bay leaves

3 flat-leaf parsley sprigs

2 thyme sprigs

1 teaspoon white wine vinegar

5 black peppercorns

generous pinch of sea salt flakes

DF, GF | MAKES 2 LITRES

Place all the ingredients in a stockpot and pour in 3 litres of cold water. Bring to the boil, then reduce the heat to low and simmer gently, occasionally skimming off the scum that rises to the surface, for 3 hours.

Strain the chicken stock through a sieve into a bowl and discard the solids. Store in an airtight container in the fridge for up to 5 days or freeze for up to 3 months.

Vegetable Stock

1 green apple, quartered
(adds body to the stock)

2 large carrots, cut into thirds

2 large celery stalks, cut into thirds

2 leeks, washed well and
roughly chopped

2 fresh bay leaves

2 garlic cloves, bashed and peeled

3 flat-leaf parsley sprigs

2 thyme sprigs

5 black peppercorns

generous pinch of sea salt flakes

DF, GF, VG | **MAKES 2 LITRES**

Place all the ingredients in a stockpot and pour in 2.25 litres of cold water. Bring to the boil, then reduce the heat to low and simmer gently for 1 hour.

Strain the vegetable stock through a sieve into a bowl and discard the solids. Store in an airtight container in the fridge for up to 5 days or freeze for up to 3 months.

Fish Stock

1 kg white fish bones

1 large carrot, cut into thirds

1 large onion, halved

1 large celery stalk, cut into thirds

2 fresh bay leaves

2 garlic cloves, bashed and peeled

3 flat-leaf parsley sprigs

5 black peppercorns

DF, GF | **MAKES 2 LITRES**

Place all the ingredients in a stockpot and pour in 2.25 litres of cold water. Bring to the boil, then reduce the heat to low and simmer gently for 1 hour.

Strain the fish stock through a sieve into a bowl and discard the solids. Store in an airtight container in the fridge for up to 3 days or freeze for up to 2 months.

GARLICKY DIPS

Skordalia
Garlic Potato Dip

500 g all-purpose potatoes
(such as sebago), peeled and
cut into 3 cm cubes

sea salt flakes and freshly ground
white pepper

2 garlic cloves, crushed

2 tablespoons white wine vinegar

125 ml (½ cup) extra-virgin olive oil

DF, GF, VG | MAKES 2 CUPS

Place the potato in a saucepan, add cold water to cover and a pinch of sea salt. Bring to a simmer over low heat and cook for 15 minutes or until the potato is tender. Drain, reserving about 125 ml (½ cup) of the starchy cooking water.

Transfer the hot potato to a food processor, add the garlic, vinegar and a pinch of salt and white pepper and blitz to combine. With the motor running, slowly pour in the olive oil and 3 tablespoons of the reserved starchy cooking water to create a silky mash. Add a little more of the water if the dip is very thick. Store in an airtight container in the fridge for up to 2 days.

Tzatziki
Garlic Yoghurt Dip

1 Lebanese cucumber, halved
lengthways and deseeded

1 teaspoon sea salt flakes

300 g Greek yoghurt
(or coconut yoghurt)

1 garlic clove, crushed

1 tablespoon white wine vinegar

1 tablespoon extra-virgin olive oil

1 tablespoon finely chopped
dill fronds

DFO, GF, V, VGO | MAKES 2 CUPS

Grate the cucumber into a colander and sprinkle on the salt. Sit for 10 minutes, then firmly squeeze out the moisture.

Place the cucumber in a bowl, add the remaining ingredients and stir to combine. Store in an airtight container in the fridge for up to 3 days.

Toum
Garlic Dip

1 head of garlic, cloves peeled

2 teaspoons sea salt flakes, plus extra if needed

250 ml (1 cup) light olive oil

1 egg white

juice of 1 lemon, plus extra if needed

DF, GF, V | MAKES 2 CUPS

Place the garlic, salt and 2 tablespoons of the olive oil in a food processor and blitz to form a coarse garlic paste (this will take a couple of minutes as you will need to stop and scrape down the side of the bowl several times). Add the egg white and whiz until light and airy. With the motor running, very slowly drizzle in the remaining olive oil until you have a creamy mixture. Add the lemon juice and whiz again to combine. Taste and add more salt or lemon juice, if required. Store in an airtight container in the fridge for up to 5 days.

OTHER DIPS

Taramasalata
Fish Roe Dip

200 g all-purpose potatoes (such as sebago), peeled and cut into 3 cm cubes

pinch of sea salt flakes

100 g tarama fish roe

½ small red onion, grated

juice of 1 lemon, plus extra if needed

pinch of freshly ground white pepper

170 ml (⅔ cup) light olive oil

DF, GF | MAKES 2 CUPS

Place the potato in a saucepan, add cold water to cover and the salt. Bring to a simmer over low heat and cook for 15 minutes or until the potato is tender. Drain, reserving 3 tablespoons of the starchy cooking water. Set aside to cool for 10 minutes.

Add the fish roe, onion, lemon juice, white pepper and potato to a food processor and blitz until just combined. With the motor running, slowly drizzle in the olive oil until smooth. To loosen the dip, pour in the reserved starchy cooking water and whiz until the dip is light and fluffy. Taste and adjust with more lemon juice, if required. Store in an airtight container in the fridge for up to 5 days.

Fava
Yellow Split Pea Dip

165 g (¾ cup) dried yellow split peas

boiling water, to cover

80 ml (⅓ cup) extra-virgin olive oil

1 small carrot, roughly chopped

1 small red onion, roughly chopped

1 celery stalk, roughly chopped

1 garlic clove, bashed and peeled

2 fresh bay leaves

sea salt flakes

625 ml (2½ cups) Vegetable Stock (page 207)

squeeze of lemon juice

DF, GF, VG | **MAKES 2 CUPS**

Place the split peas in a bowl, pour over the boiling water to cover, stir and set aside to soak for 10 minutes. Drain and rinse the peas.

Combine the olive oil, carrot, onion, celery, garlic, bay leaves and a good pinch of salt in a saucepan and place over medium–low heat. Sauté, stirring occasionally, for 8 minutes to soften. Add the split peas and vegetable stock and bring to the boil. Reduce the heat to low and simmer, stirring regularly, for 25 minutes or until the split peas soften. Discard the bay leaves and transfer the split pea mixture to a food processor. Add the lemon juice and blitz to a creamy puree (the dip will thicken as it cools). Store in an airtight container in the fridge for up to 5 days.

Hummus

250 g dried chickpeas

1 teaspoon bicarbonate of soda

180 g (⅔ cup) tahini

3 tablespoons freshly squeezed lemon juice, plus extra if needed

4 garlic cloves, crushed

1 teaspoon sea salt flakes, plus extra if needed

4 ice cubes

HUMMUS TOPPINGS

fried or roasted chickpeas, pomegranate seeds, za'atar, sumac, toasted pine nuts, finely chopped flat-leaf parsley leaves

DF, GF, VG | **MAKES 2 CUPS**

Place the chickpeas and bicarbonate of soda in a large bowl, cover with water and set aside to soak overnight.

Drain the chickpeas, rinse thoroughly, then transfer to a saucepan and cover with plenty of water. Bring to a simmer over low heat and cook, skimming off any impurities and loose skins that rise to the surface, for 45–60 minutes or until the chickpeas are tender. Drain and transfer the chickpeas to a food processor.

Blitz the chickpeas to form a paste, scraping down the side of the bowl when necessary. Allow to cool for 15 minutes. Add the tahini, lemon juice, garlic, salt and ice cubes and whiz for 3–5 minutes or until the hummus is smooth and creamy. Taste and adjust the seasoning with more lemon juice or salt, if required. Serve with the toppings of your choice. Store in an airtight container in the fridge for up to 5 days.

Melitzanosalata
Eggplant Dip

2 large eggplants

3 tablespoons extra-virgin olive oil

3 garlic cloves, crushed

2 tablespoons red wine vinegar

handful of flat-leaf parsley leaves, finely chopped

pinch of sea salt flakes and freshly ground black pepper

DF, GF, VG | **MAKES 2 CUPS**

Cook the eggplants directly over an open flame for 10 minutes, turning regularly until the skin is charred and blistered. Place the eggplants in a heatproof bowl, cover with plastic wrap and allow to cool.

When the eggplants are cool enough to handle, peel away the skin and place the flesh in a sieve set over a bowl. Press down firmly to strain the liquid from the eggplant flesh into the bowl. Discard the liquid and transfer the eggplant flesh to a food processor. Add the remaining ingredients and blitz to a coarse puree. Taste and adjust the seasoning as required. Store in an airtight container in the fridge for up to 5 days.

Tahini Sauce

135 g (½ cup) tahini

80 ml (⅓ cup) freshly squeezed lemon juice

2 garlic cloves, finely chopped

pinch of sea salt flakes

DF, GF, VG | **MAKES 1 CUP**

Place all the ingredients in a bowl and whisk together to form a thick paste. Whisking continuously, slowly drizzle in some water until the sauce is creamy and runny. Taste and adjust the seasoning as required. Store in an airtight container in the fridge for up to 1 week.

Conversion charts

Measuring cups and spoons may vary slightly from one country to another, but the difference is generally not enough to affect a recipe. All cup and spoon measures are level.

One Australian metric measuring cup holds 250 ml (8 fl oz), one Australian metric tablespoon holds 20 ml (4 teaspoons) and one Australian metric teaspoon holds 5 ml. North America, New Zealand and the UK use a 15 ml (3-teaspoon) tablespoon.

LENGTH

METRIC	IMPERIAL
3 mm	⅛ inch
6 mm	¼ inch
1 cm	½ inch
2.5 cm	1 inch
5 cm	2 inches
18 cm	7 inches
20 cm	8 inches
23 cm	9 inches
25 cm	10 inches
30 cm	12 inches

LIQUID MEASURES

ONE AMERICAN PINT	ONE IMPERIAL PINT
500 ml (16 fl oz)	600 ml (20 fl oz)

CUP	METRIC	IMPERIAL
⅛ cup	30 ml	1 fl oz
¼ cup	60 ml	2 fl oz
⅓ cup	80 ml	2½ fl oz
½ cup	125 ml	4 fl oz
⅔ cup	160 ml	5 fl oz
¾ cup	180 ml	6 fl oz
1 cup	250 ml	8 fl oz
2 cups	500 ml	16 fl oz
2¼ cups	560 ml	20 fl oz
4 cups	1 litre	32 fl oz

DRY MEASURES

The most accurate way to measure dry ingredients is to weigh them. However, if using a cup, add the ingredient loosely to the cup and level with a knife; don't compact the ingredient unless the recipe requests 'firmly packed'.

METRIC	IMPERIAL
15 g	½ oz
30 g	1 oz
60 g	2 oz
125 g	4 oz (¼ lb)
185 g	6 oz
250 g	8 oz (½ lb)
375 g	12 oz (¾ lb)
500 g	16 oz (1 lb)
1 kg	32 oz (2 lb)

OVEN TEMPERATURES

CELSIUS	FAHRENHEIT
100°C	200°F
120°C	250°F
150°C	300°F
160°C	325°F
180°C	350°F
200°C	400°F
220°C	425°F

CELSIUS	GAS MARK
110°C	¼
130°C	½
140°C	1
150°C	2
170°C	3
180°C	4
190°C	5
200°C	6
220°C	7
230°C	8
240°C	9
250°C	10

Thank you

Mary, Clare, Jeremy and Vanessa. This is our second book together and once again you have been an absolute dream to work with. Always supportive, collaborative, kind and encouraging. Thank you for giving me the opportunity to bring my rustic, romantic Mediterranean vision to life. I could not have asked for a better team and I'm so proud of what we have created together.

To the food team, Lucy, Vikki and Theressa. It was an absolute joy cooking alongside you and sharing tips on everything from the best lemon zesters to parenting teenagers while covered in pasta sauce and flour. Thank you for working so hard to keep the busy shoot on schedule. I had loads of fun in the kitchen with you and hope we can swap more tips in future.

Megan, thank you for your beautiful words and eagle eye. I'm glad you enjoyed sampling some of the bikkies while editing. Emily, your stunning design and illustrations perfectly capture the essence and mood of Mediterranean cooking, so thank you.

To the sales, marketing and publicity teams at Pan Macmillan, thank you for working so hard to get this book into as many hands as possible.

To Coeliac Australia, thank you for your endorsement and for being an invaluable resource for coeliacs in Australia.

To my immediate family, Spiro, Vasili, Sofia and Ruby, and extended family and friends. I cherish your wholehearted love, support and words of encouragement. Thank you for being my taste testers and for giving me the best advice ever when recipe testing and culling: 'If it's not something you would cook for us again and again, why would you include it?' So true, Vasili. Sometimes you need a kid's brutal honesty to keep you on the right track!

Finally, thank you to everyone who has purchased this book. None of this would be possible without your continued support. I truly hope this becomes your go-to practical family cookbook, the one with all the scribbled notes, crumpled pages and oil spills. Nothing makes me happier than seeing someone cook my recipes, so please share your creations on social media with pride – I love seeing your photos. I hope these recipes become treasured family heirlooms that form the basis of beautiful food memories in your home too.

Lots of love,
Helen

Index

Pan Macmillan acknowledges the Traditional Custodians of Country throughout Australia and their connections to lands, waters and communities. We pay our respect to Elders past and present and extend that respect to all Aboriginal and Torres Strait Islander peoples today. We honour more than sixty thousand years of storytelling, art and culture.

A PLUM book
First published in 2023 by
Pan Macmillan Australia Pty Limited
Level 25, 1 Market Street,
Sydney, NSW 2000, Australia

Level 3, 112 Wellington Parade,
East Melbourne, VIC 3002, Australia

Text copyright © Helen Tzouganatos 2023
Photographs Jeremy Simons copyright © Pan Macmillan 2023
Design Emily O'Neill copyright © Pan Macmillan 2023

Designed, illustrated and typeset by Emily O'Neill
Edited by Megan Johnston
Index by Helena Holmgren
Photography by Jeremy Simons
Food and prop styling by Vanessa Austin
Food preparation by Lucy Busuttil, Theressa Klein,
    Vikki Moursellas and Helen Tzouganatos
Colour reproduction by Splitting Image Colour Studio
Printed and bound in China by Hang Tai Printing Co. Ltd.

A CIP catalogue record for this book is available from
the National Library of Australia.

10 9 8 7 6 5 4 3 2 1

ENDORSED BY COELIAC AUSTRALIA
GLUTEN FREE